THE
FINAL
HOUR

UNDERSTANDING WHAT THE BIBLE HAS TO SAY ABOUT THE END TIMES

MARILYN HICKEY

Harrison Hou

D0005571

20 21 22 23   10 9 8 7 6 5
The Final Hour: Understanding What the Bible Says About the End Times
ISBN 978-168031-071-9
Copyright © 2004,2016 by Marilyn Hickey Ministries P. O. Box 17340
Denver, CO 8021 7

Published by Harrison House Publishers
167 Walnut Bottom Rd
Shippensburg, PA 17257

CONTENTS

SECTION 4 END-TIME EVENTS

SECTION 5 THE MILLENNIUM

INTRODUCTION

Is America—and the world—poised at a defining moment in history? Are the nations of the world forming political alliances for the fulfillment of end-time prophecies? Are we approaching the end of the world as we know it? That is not only a very great concern of Christians, but of backslidden Christians, Buddhists, and Muslims, literally people all around the world.

There is no question that our world is rushing headlong toward the "last days," because sometimes reading the paper is like reading the Bible. Present-day headlines could have been written by Bible prophets thousands of years ago. How could anyone not think that we are approaching the end of the world? However, it is not a season to fear but a time to rejoice. Jesus said that when these things start happening, we're to look up because the Rapture (our redemption) is near. (Luke 21:28.)

The original Greek for *Rapture* has to do with catching away, but not everyone is going to be "caught up," only those believers who are ready.

This is wrap-up time. It's wind-up time. The Rapture could occur at any moment. That's why I believe that this is the season for us to preach the Rapture and teach Bible prophecy. I believe it is the season for Christians to know what is going on and what their role is so they'll be ready when the Rapture occurs. Jesus said, "Don't be troubled" (Matt. 24:6), but you're going to be troubled if you don't know the truth. In Hosea 4:6 we're told, "My people [or Christians] are destroyed for lack of knowledge...." But if you know the truth, you're not going to be troubled because you're going to be looking in the right place.

LOOK FOR HIM

The terrorist attack of September 11, 2003, has changed our world. This shocking event has polarized the nations into a struggle between good and evil, thus, setting the world stage for the "end times." The Rapture, the Antichrist, the Tribulation, Armageddon, the defeat of Satan, and the beginning of Christ's reign upon the earth are all end-time events that will be covered in this book.

As we will see, the Bible books of prophecy teach that the Antichrist will try to rule the entire world, but before he takes power, millions of Christians—*but not all*—will be removed from our planet. We need to make certain that we are part of the group that is leaving first, the "overcoming church." The lukewarm church will *not* go to heaven in this pre-tribulation Rapture. They must endure three-and-a-half years of the darkest, most difficult period in human history—the second half of the Tribulation.

The battle of Armageddon will be the most terrible battle the world has ever known. Tens—and perhaps hundreds—of thousands of people will die. The Bible says that there has never been, nor will there ever be, a battle so great.

In the final moments of the war, all will seem to be lost and the Antichrist will appear to have won—to have defeated Israel and her allies. Then, Jesus Christ will break through the clouds to return to earth with an army of saints. Christ Himself will defeat Satan, the Antichrist, and their horde.

Where will you be in that day?

When you become born again, there is no question where your destination is, where you are going. The Bible promises that you're going to go to heaven, but it doesn't promise you that you are going to make the first Rapture. Whether that happens or not has to do with your decision. So if you miss the first Rapture, that doesn't mean you're going to miss heaven, because if you have Jesus in your heart, you are going to heaven. But every Christian is not going in the first Rapture.

Some believers may want to dream that up and think it, but it's just not in the Bible. Jesus is coming for those who are looking for Him, and some Christians are not looking for anything but a new car or another woman or another man or another drink.

The purpose of this book is to prepare you to be Rapture ready by illustrating God's plan for the end times and where you fit into it. When you get saved, you're promised heaven. But you make your choice of which Rapture you're going to go in. If you're not taught the Word and what God says, then you won't know the truth. But if you know the truth and you know what it is to be ready for the Rapture, and you decide that you're going to miss the Tribulation, that is your choice.

WHERE IS YOUR WALK?

This is not going to be a depressing message, but it is a serious message because this is a serious time we're living in. Thousands of years ago God wrote about this time in His Word so that when we would be living in it, we wouldn't be ignorant or afraid when we see these things happen. He wanted us to know that when we have His Son Jesus inside of us, we're not a part of Satan's plan; we're a part of his ultimate defeat.

But many people don't like to study prophecy. It's confusing to them because they read some of it in Ezekiel, they read some in Daniel and in Zechariah, they read the book of Revelation, they read the three chapters in the Gospels that are very prophetic, and they think, *What piece goes where, and how does this all fit together?*

We'll be studying end-time prophecy in this book, and I've written it so you will understand it. I want it to be simple for you. I don't want you to put this book down and say, "This is confusing. My brain is scrambled. I don't know if I can get all this." I want you to say, "I see it. It's in the Word. It's clear," so that by the time you finish reading, you will know if you are ready for the pretribulation Rapture or not. There won't be any question in your mind; you will know.

Even if you can just get pieces of it, it will help you to know if you are part of the overcoming church or the slop along church. It will help you to know that this is the revelation of Jesus Christ and who is the true and living God. It will help you to know that we win.

I believe that as you look at this book, the Holy Spirit is going to help and encourage you, but also exhort you and challenge you, on where your walk is in God. Our world has become too dangerous a place to be lukewarm in your relationship with Him and possibly miss the Rapture. So I pray that your heart will be very sensitive to God as you read on, that He will give you revelation knowledge and open the eyes of your understanding so you will see what He has for you in this message.

SECTION 1

PURPOSE AND PLAN

CHAPTER 1

ARE YOU WATCHING?

"Watch therefore, for you do not know what hour your
Lord is coming."

Matthew 24:42 NKJV

Can you imagine if you were working with somebody
and that person just suddenly disappeared? What if you
were in bed with your mate and you *weren't* a Christian, and
your mate suddenly vanished and you were left there. You
would probably think, *Where are they?* Or what if you *were*
a Christian and the same thing happened? It would be very
frightening—and the Rapture will happen like that.

When the Rapture takes place will be very secret, and
that's a prime factor. In Matthew 24:36,40-41, the Bible tells
us about "that day" and how it will just suddenly happen: "But
of that day and hour knoweth no man, no, not the angels of
heaven, but My Father only....Then shall two be in the field;
the one shall be taken, and the other left. Two women shall be
grinding at the mill; the one shall be taken, and the other left."

Angels don't know when. Nobody knows the hour; nobody knows the day. It's a surprise.

> But ye, brethren, are not in darkness, that that day should overtake you as a thief.
>
> 1 Thessalonians 5:4

It's not D-day, VJ-day, but that day, and one-third of the Bible is directed toward this. I don't know when the Rapture is coming, but there are signs to help me know that it is soon and truths in God's Word to help me to be ready when it comes. From the Word, we do know about some of the events and conditions that will be going on in that time. These are signs to make us aware.

> "But as the days of Noah were, so also will the coming of the Son of Man be.
>
> "For as in the days before the flood, they were eating and drinking, marrying and giving in marriage, until the day that Noah entered the ark,
>
> "and did not know until the flood came and took them all away, so also will the coming of the Son of Man be."
>
> Matthew 24:37-39 NKJV

We will look at this more later on, but it will be life as usual. People will be eating, drinking, getting married. It won't be, "Oh, things are bad. They're terrible." There won't be big signs in the heavens at that moment. It will be very ordinary times. You may be getting up, fixing breakfast, going out for coffee, doing whatever you usually do. It will be a very normal time. But Luke 21:34 says, "And take heed to yourselves, lest at any time your hearts be overcharged with surfeiting and drunkenness, and cares of this life...."

Surfeiting is related to partying; someone who is out having parties, drinking and eating too much, and living it up.[1] Now I doubt that most believers are partying all the time or that they're drunk a lot of the time, but they may be caught up in the "cares of this life." That could be pressure, and so many people are under pressure and not casting their cares upon the Lord. "And so that day come upon you unawares" (v. 34), because they're just thinking, *Well, it's life as usual, and I'm just doing my thing. I don't have much of a focus on God. Oh yes, I'm a Christian. I love Jesus, but I'm busy.*

In Matthew 24:42 Jesus gave us the big key to making the Rapture: "Watch...." Again, in Luke 21:36, He says, "*Watch* ye therefore, and pray always, that ye may be accounted worthy to escape all these things that shall come to pass, and to stand before the Son of man."

You have to be watching for Jesus' return because the Rapture has a purpose—it's to get you out of here before things get bad.

> **Because thou hast kept the word of my patience, I also will keep thee from the hour of temptation, which shall come upon all the world, to try them that dwell upon the earth.**
> **Revelation 3:10**

This verse doesn't sound as though every Christian is going in the first Rapture. It sounds as though the ones going first are people who are watching for Jesus' second coming and who have a godly lifestyle. They love Jesus. They're trying to serve Him, and He is saying, "I want to get you out of here before these terrible things begin to come to pass because they're going to be really rough."

ATTITUDE IS EVERYTHING

"But know this, that if the master of the house had known what hour the thief would come, he would have watched and not allowed his house to be broken into.

"Therefore you also be ready, for the Son of Man is coming at an hour you do not expect.

"Who then is a faithful and wise servant, whom his master made ruler over his household, to give them food in due season?

"Blessed is that servant whom his master, when he comes, will find so doing."

Matthew 24:43-46 NKJV

In this passage, Jesus is telling about a certain servant and what he is doing—he's watching; he's looking in the right place. Jesus says of him, "Assuredly, I say to you that he will make him ruler over all his goods..." (v. 47 NKJV).

Jesus continues, "...But if that evil servant says in his heart, 'My master is delaying his coming,' and begins to beat his fellow servants, and to eat and drink with the drunkards" (vv. 48,49 NKJV). What happens to the evil servant? He gets in a wrong attitude about what's going on.

We can have the same kind of attitude about what's going on today. We can think, *Oh well, I've heard Jesus is coming for years. So big deal. Al-Qaida and other terrorist groups are out there; I don't think that has anything to do with Jesus. Some in government are trying to form a worldwide coalition, which could present the Antichrist. That doesn't mean the Rapture is going to come. I don't know if anything is going on,* and just live any old common lifestyle. It doesn't have to be extremely sinful, but just the common cares of the world or the attitude, "I don't care," could be very dangerous at this time.

This is due season. This is not the time to have a bad attitude. It's not the time to get mad at your friends or relatives or anyone else. This is a bad time to do that. Don't get into bitterness and ugliness and quit going to church. This is the time we must keep the right attitude and stay committed to the things of God.

Notice what Jesus said in Matthew 24:50-51 NKJV: "The master of that servant will come on a day when he is not looking for him and at an hour that he is not aware of, and will cut him in two and appoint him his portion with the hypocrites. There shall be weeping and gnashing of teeth."

Jesus didn't say that he was going to hell, but said he's acting like a hypocrite. So attitude is very important. The wrong attitude is a dangerous attitude.

Sometimes when I wake up in the morning, I just like to have a bad attitude. Do you ever feel that way? Perhaps you felt, *I just deserve to have a bad attitude. I'm tired and I have all of these pressures. I deserve to be ugly today. This is my ugly day. I'm going to snap at people. I'm going to be ugly to people today. This is my bad attitude today.* We can't afford bad attitude days now. We've got to stay in a godly attitude.

A dangerous attitude is a wicked attitude when someone says, "I've heard that Jesus is coming, but I don't know that any thing is going to happen. We've heard these things for years." I've had people say this to me, and you probably have too; maybe you've even said it yourself. But 2 Peter 3:3-4 tells us that people like this are going to be around in the last days: "Knowing this first, that there shall come in the last days scoffers, walking after their own lusts, and saying, Where is the promise of his coming? for since the fathers fell asleep, all things continue as they were from the beginning of the creation."

There are going to be scoffers like this in the last days, and they're not going to make the first Rapture. But you're going to have to make a choice. Are you going to listen to scoffers? Are you going to be a scoffer? I don't think you'd be reading this book about the Rapture if you were much of a scoffer. I think you must be very passionate for Jesus.

CHASING AFTER JESUS

You could have a fairly good lifestyle and a right attitude, but there's something else you need to be doing. Are you looking for Jesus? Are you passionate for Him? When you worship Him and love Him, does it make your heart hungry for more of Him? Do you want to see Him, not just to get out of here, to get away from a mean wife or ugly husband, but because you love Him and you want to be with Him? We need to have a relationship with Him that says, "I love Jesus. He talks to me. I talk to Him. He's my Savior. He died for me. I'm very aware of His Presence, and I'm watching for His return."

Watch is used in many places in Scripture, and there are a lot of different Greek and Hebrew words for *watch*. But this particular use of *watch* that I'm talking about only occurs four times in the Bible, and it has very special meaning. It tells us how to watch.

When Jesus says, "Watch," what do we do, walk out every morning and look up? I can imagine someone doing that and saying, *My neighbors think I'm crazy. I'm always standing out looking up . At work, I run out at lunchtime and just look up. When I get out of my car, I'm always looking up. People ask me, "Do you have a problem with your neck?"* Of course, that's not what Jesus means! So how do we *watch*?

This word *watch* means, "to be sleepless, keep awake...To be circumspect, attentive, ready."[2] In other words, stay alert. It also means to follow; to chase.[3] There's a tremendous book written by popular pastor and author Tommy Tenney called, *God Chasers: "My Soul Follows Hard After Thee.*"[4] That is so passionate to me. This *watch* means that we're chasing after Jesus. Let's look at the four places in the Bible where it occurs.

We've already seen it in Luke 21:36. "Watch ye therefore... " or chase after Jesus, keep chasing Him, stay alert, stay awake, pray always, so that you'll escape these things. This is especially an intense watch. This is the only *watch* in the Bible that means to chase, as in chasing after Jesus.

I love Hebrews 13:17 where this *watch* also appears.

> "Obey them that have the rule over you, and submit yourselves: for they watch for your souls, as they that must give account, that they may do it with joy, and not with grief: for that is unprofitable for you."

This verse is saying that people who are in Christian leadership should be watching over their people to see that they're watching for Jesus. They should be bugging you to get in your Bible. You may be tired of hearing them tell you that, but we're chasing after you to make sure that you are in the first Rapture. We don't want you going through the Tribulation.

Look at the next time *watch* appears. Mark 13:33 says, "Take ye heed, watch and pray: for ye know not when the time is."

In other words, be careful. Keep chasing Jesus. Keep alert. Stay awake because you don't know when the time of His return could be. Could it be in the next 24 hours? Could it be in the next 24 days? We've got enough signs that it could be.

So what are we doing when we are watching? Our lifestyle is chasing after Jesus. It's not just looking up. It's chasing after Him. That means being awake, and according to Ephesians 6:18, we're not just awake for ourselves and chasing Him for ourselves, but we're concerned about the rest of the body of Christ.

> **Praying always with all prayer and supplication in the Spirit,** *and watching thereunto with all perseverance and supplication for all saints.*

This verse says that we're to be watching and chasing after people so that they hang in and hang tight with God. For example, if you don't see somebody at church, call them.

I believe that something awesome is happening in these last days, and people are beginning to chase after Jesus as never before. These are people from all kinds of churches, not just from Pentecostal, Charismatic churches, and we must watch for them and pray them in, in this special time.

MISSION OR COMMISSION?

We are absolutely in a dark time, and Matthew 25 implies that Jesus is coming in the dark time of the world. In that chapter He gives one picture after another of the Rapture and of being ready for it.

"Then the kingdom of heaven shall be likened to ten virgins who took their lamps and went out to meet the bridegroom.

"Now five of them were wise, and five were foolish.

"Those who were foolish took their lamps and took no oil with them,

"but the wise took oil in their vessels with their lamps.

"But while the bridegroom was delayed, they all slumbered and slept.

"And at midnight a cry was heard: 'Behold, the bridegroom is coming; go out to meet him!'

"Then all those virgins arose and trimmed their lamps.

"And the foolish said to the wise, 'Give us some of your oil, for our lamps are going out.'

"But the wise answered, saying, 'No, lest there should not be enough for us and you; but go rather to those who sell, and buy for yourselves.'

"And while they went to buy, the bridegroom came, and those who were ready went in with him to the wedding; and the door was shut.

"Afterward the other virgins came also, saying, 'Lord, Lord, open to us!'

"But he answered and said, 'Assuredly, I say to you, I do not know you.'

"*Watch* therefore, for you know neither the day nor the hour in which the Son of Man is coming."

Matthew 25:1-13 NKJV

This passage tells of another attitude we have to be very careful with in this time. What is it about these five foolish virgins that caused them to miss the bridegroom? Were they big sinners? Were they out drinking? Were they out smoking dope or taking heroin? Were they out committing adultery? Were they sleeping with somebody else's spouse? No, this passage doesn't say that. It says that they were lazy and indifferent and let the fire go out; they let the oil go out. To them, it was a mission, not a commission.

How does that relate to us? You may say, "My favorite football team is playing Sunday morning. I can't go to church." Or, "I've got unsaved relatives in town, and we're going to the mountains on Sunday." Or, "My kids have sports on Sundays. You'll just have to miss me one or two Sundays a month." Or, "I have a home in the mountains now, and we worship God in the mountains." Well, I know you don't call to the mountains for help when you get in trouble! Don't do it; they won't help you.

That's an attitude of omission, and this is a dangerous time to be spending your Sundays in the mountains or watching the football games instead of going to church. You'd better be in the house of God and tape the ball game. This is not a time to play around.

Now I didn't write this; God did. But I sure want to live by it. How about you?

PROFITABLE AND PRODUCING

Let's go a little further in Matthew 25, beginning at verse 14. This passage also has to do with lifestyle and being ready for the Rapture. Jesus says,

> "For the kingdom of heaven is like a man traveling to a far country, who called his own servants and delivered his goods to them.
>
> "And to one he gave five talents, to another two, and to another one, to each according to his own ability; and immediately he went on a journey.
>
> "Then he who had received the five talents went and traded with them, and made another five talents.
>
> "And likewise he who had received two gained two more also.
>
> "But he who had received one went and dug in the ground, and hid his lord's money.
>
> "After a long time the lord of those servants came and settled accounts with them.

"So he who had received five talents came and brought five other talents, saying, 'Lord, you delivered to me five talents; look, I have gained five more talents besides them.'

"His lord said to him, 'Well done, good and faithful servant; you were faithful over a few things, I will make you ruler over many things. Enter into the joy of your lord.'

"He also who had received two talents came and said, 'Lord, you delivered to me two talents; look, I have gained two more talents besides them.'

"His lord said to him, 'Well done, good and faithful servant; you have been faithful over a few things, I will make you ruler over many things. Enter into the joy of your lord.'

"Then he who had received the one talent came and said, 'Lord, I knew you to be a hard man, reaping where you have not sown, and gathering where you have not scattered seed.

'And I was afraid, and went and hid your talent in the ground. Look, there you have what is yours.'

"But his lord answered and said to him, 'You wicked and lazy servant, you knew that I reap where I have not sown, and gather where I have not scattered seed.

'So you ought to have deposited my money with the bankers, and at my coming I would have received back my own with interest.

'Therefore take the talent from him, and give it to him who has ten talents.

'For to everyone who has, more will be given, and he will have abundance; but from him who does not have, even what he has will be taken away.

'And cast the unprofitable servant into the outer darkness. There will be weeping and gnashing of teeth.'

"When the Son of Man comes in His glory.... "

Matthew 25:14-31 NKJV

What is your lifestyle? Are you producing anything for the kingdom at all? Are you like the profitable servant or the unprofitable servant in this passage? You may say, "Well, God's been so good. He's saved me and filled me with the Holy Ghost, and He's blessed me, and some of my family are saved." But what are you doing for God?

Are you just laid back, slopping around, having fun and doing nothing in the kingdom? That is not the kind of people who are going to be in the first Rapture. When Jesus comes, He is coming for profitable servants. Who is profitable? People who are producing—not perfect people, but producing people.

In these passages Jesus gives us an overall picture. He spends a lot of time just on the Rapture itself because He wants everybody to make the first Rapture. He doesn't want anybody to miss it. He hasn't appointed us to wrath. He doesn't want the devil to beat us into a pulp. He doesn't want us to take the mark of the beast or be beheaded because we're serving Him. He wants us out of here.

WILD ABOUT YOU

Do you know what Jesus' purpose is for the Rapture? It's to get you. He wants to receive you unto Himself, that where He is, you'll be there also. In fact, Jesus is just wild to get His hands on you. That is reflected in one of the meanings of *rapture,* which is "to...claim for one's self eagerly." [5]

I remember when my daughter, Sarah, was born. When I was in the delivery room, my husband, Wally, said to me, "It's a girl," and my first thought was, *It's over.* Then they took me back to the room, and I was asleep because they had given me something. But when I awakened, I said, "Bring me my baby. I want to see my baby." I could hardly wait to get my hands on her. So the nurse went and got this little baby girl. She was all wrapped in a blanket really tight, and I unwrapped her. I looked at every little finger. I looked at every little toe. I looked at her eyes, her ears, her hair, everything about her. Then I hugged her and loved her. What did I do? I claimed her as my own.

That's what the Rapture is—when Jesus unwraps you, counts your little fingers and your toes, squeezes you to Himself, and says, "You're Mine. I've got you." The Rapture is to claim you for Himself.

HINDERING THE ENEMY

Jesus wants you to escape the terrible things in the Tribulation that are coming because He loves you. But until you get out of here, the Antichrist can't be revealed, because the Scripture says, "For the mystery of iniquity doth already work. Only he who now letteth will let, until he be taken out of the way" (2 Thess. 2:7). Using the word *allow* instead of *let* will help you better understand what this verse is saying.

"For the mystery of iniquity doth already work. Only he who now *alloweth* will *allow*, until he be taken out of the way."

What do you think hinders the devil from doing everything he wants to do? Point to yourself and say, *I do. My prayers hinder the devil. When I get out of here, he'll have more freedom.* When Jesus takes us out, then the Antichrist can rise up. As long as the overcoming church is here, the Antichrist cannot come on the scene because we bind the devil. We take the Word and speak it. We know how to use the name of Jesus. We know that we overcome by the blood of the Lamb, the word of our testimony, and our lifestyle, that we love not our lives unto death. (Rev. 12:11.) God's got a purpose for this.

God didn't just wake up one day and say, "Oh, I'm going to have a Rapture." He always has a plan. He always has a purpose. He never is shocked. He has had all these things in the Bible for years. People didn't understand Him. They believed these things, but they didn't understand them. But now we're living in them, so if any generation ought to understand them, we should. The big thing is, *are you ready?*

ARE YOU A WATCHER?

We saw earlier that one meaning of *watch* is to chase, so if I could put it simply, I would say that Jesus is coming for watchers or God chasers. Does that describe you? If you're not sure, ask yourself these questions.

Am I aware that the Rapture is secret and sudden?

Am I aware that life will be going on as usual when it happens, that people will be marrying, eating, drinking? You know, your cousin may be getting married or people may be coming over for Christmas. You'll be getting the punch bowl down, and Jesus will come, and the punch bowl will fall on the floor and break because you'll go up in the Rapture.

Am I aware that it will be an escape from the worst evil the world has ever known? Before September 11, 2001, we might not have thought about the worst evil, but I think now we're quite aware.

Do I have a good relationship with God? Does He talk to me? Do I listen when He talks? Do I talk to Him? Do I know His sweetness? Am I aware that He Loves me? I like what Jesus said about that in John 15:9 ESV. He said, "As the Father has loved Me, so have I loved you. Abide in My love." If you're doing that, you can just relax.

When you know that someone loves you, you can kick off your shoes and be relaxed with them because they love you. Even if you didn't take a bath and your feet stink, they love you. Jesus wants us to abide in His love. A watcher is not abiding in, "I've got to do this and I've got to do that." He's abiding in Jesus' love because he's after Him. If you're after Jesus, you'll know He loves you.

Am I faithful in God's house? Christians can be foolish about their walk with God in such a serious time, just as the five foolish virgins were. *Am I faithful? Is my present life preparing me for eternal life? Is my lifestyle preparing me for a lifestyle with Him forever?* This is not ritual, but relationship. Romans 13:11-14 NKJV is a passage that helps me to know how to have a good relationship with God.

> And do this, knowing the time, that now it is high time to awake out of sleep; for now our salvation is nearer than when we first believed.
>
> The night is far spent, the day is at hand. Therefore let us cast off the works of darkness, and let us put on the armor of light.
>
> Let us walk properly, as in the day, not in revelry and drunkenness, not in lewdness and lust, not in strife and envy.
>
> But put on the Lord Jesus Christ, and make no provision for the flesh, to fulfill its lusts.

So what are we going to do? We're going to watch, we're going to chase after Jesus, because those are the people who are going in the first Rapture.

CHAPTER 2

SIGNS OF HIS RETURN

And as he sat upon the mount of Olives, the disciples
came unto him privately, saying, Tell us, when shall these
things be? and what shall be the sign of thy coming, and
of the end of the world?

Matthew 24:3

All Bible prophecy has to do with three major arenas—
the Jews, the church, and the nations. As we continue
to look at Matthew 24, we are going to see what Jesus has to
say to each of these on the end times.

Basically what we have in that chapter is the future of the
church, the Jews, the Rapture, the return of Christ, and the
judgment of the nations. It takes what's in Isaiah, Ezekiel, Daniel, and Revelation and begins to put it all in one package, giving
us a crisp, condensed look at the whole end-times picture.

The chapter starts with four of the disciples asking Jesus
three questions, which really are on everybody's heart. He
answers the three questions and wraps the whole thing in
one box.

Jesus had just told the disciples that one stone was not going to be left on another of the temple, that one day the whole building would be knocked down. (Matt. 24:2.) So they were full of questions: "When is this going to start? When will the end times be? What will be the sign of the end of the age, when we are literally coming to the end of the world? How can we know it, and when are You coming back? What will be a sign of Your return?"

Notice they asked Him what would be the sign of His coming. Let's understand what coming is here. It's not just Jesus' appearing, but it's His Presence, His arrival. You will see two *comings*, two arrivals, mentioned in Matthew 24. They are very important because they are two of the Raptures. I believe that there are actually four Raptures in the Scriptures. We'll look at them later on, but the one that's the most important to you is the first one. That Rapture is when Jesus comes back for the overcoming church, when His Presence appears, His arrival.

The three sets of people He is talking to in that chapter are important because if you know whom He's talking to, you will know the reason for His statements. First of all, Jesus is going to talk to the pretribulation saints. That's you and me. He says to us, "...Take heed that no man deceive you" (v. 4). He's very concerned that before the Rapture, we don't fall for anybody's deception; we don't get off and go some crazy way and backslide and do foolish things.

Then in His second answer He says, " ...they shall lay their hands on you, and persecute you..." (Luke 21:12), because after the overcoming church goes in the Rapture, there will be terrible times upon the earth. The Antichrist will come forth and he will be revealed, and he will be cruel and terrible. He will rule a major part of the world. It will be an awful time. People will be saved in that time, because the Holy Spirit never leaves the earth, but Christians will be under terrible tribulation.

The people who go into the Tribulation obviously didn't go up in the first Rapture. "They shall lay their hands on you, and persecute you" Is His message to them—the backslidden Christians, or Christians who weren't on fire for God, who go into the Tribulation, and people who get saved in the Tribulation. It will be a hard time for born-again believers.

Then He has something to say to the Jews, because toward the end of the seven years of tribulation, there will be heavy pressure on the Jews. For a while, they will buy into the deception that the Antichrist is their messiah. But eventually they will realize that he's not the one, and he will begin to persecute them. These will be terrible times that Tribulation Jews who have received Jesus will have to endure. They've turned from the Antichrist, seeing his deception, and have turned to Jesus Christ.

DON'T WORRY

And Jesus answered and said unto them, Take heed that no man deceive you.

For many shall come in my name, saying, I am Christ; and shall deceive many.

And ye shall hear of wars and rumours of wars: see that
ye be not troubled: for all these things must come to pass,
but the end is not yet.

Matthew 24:4-6

One of the signs that we're in the pretribulation time and drawing near to the Tribulation is in Jesus' answer to "When shall these things be?" He said that there's going to be a lot of deception. People are going to say, "I'm Christ," "This is Jesus," "New Age is the way," "Get into Hinduism," "Be a Muslim." There will be many things to pull people into deception. Aren't we living in that time, a time when people are just going after every kind of kooky, flaky thing there is in the world?

But then Jesus says there's another sign—not only will false religion multiply, but also there will be a lot of wars and rumors of wars. Aren't we seeing that?

This pretribulation time will have the greatest advances of science. We're seeing that too. Just think of all the things that are available that we can do. Today's technology is so amazing that we can contact the world. But we will also see the greatest destructive power in the hands of wicked people.

There is great concern that some terrorist groups may have a nuclear bomb and certain kinds of missiles. It is also believed that some countries that favor terrorists have them, and they are closely guarding them. So these kinds of destructive power are in the hands of wicked people even now.

The greatest activity in the evil spirit world will be going on. That can be seen in what Al-Qaida (an Islamic terrorist group) did to try to overcome us on September 11, 2001. So there is no question that we're living in that time. But the Bible tells us not to be troubled.

You may say, "I watch the news. I hear all the bad things that are going on, and they are troubling." But what did Jesus say to us? In verse 6, written basically to the pretribulation church, or the overcoming church, He told us that when we see wars and all the other end-time events coming, we're to expect them, but the "...end is not yet," so don't worry.

REDEMPTION IS NEAR

And then shall they see the Son of man coming in a cloud with power and great glory.

And when these things begin to come to pass, then look up, and lift up your heads; for your redemption draweth nigh.
Luke 21:27,28

This is an awesome passage that ties right in with Matthew 24. When you see these things begin, are you supposed to be troubled, anxious, have a nervous breakdown? No, Jesus says, "Look up, your redemption draweth nigh." *Redemption* is the Rapture of the church, because redemption in that verse is Jesus taking us out and claiming us as His own.

So what should we be looking for? Some people are looking for terrorists. Some are looking at their mail to see if they've got Anthrax powder in it. Others are looking to see if they're going to lose all their money in the stock market. People are looking, looking, looking, but Jesus didn't tell us to look at those things. He told us where to look—1 "look up"—because He said, "I'm getting ready to come and get you." So when these things begin, that's *good* news.

BEGINNING OF SORROWS

All these are the beginning of sorrows.

Then shall they deliver you up to be afflicted, and shall kill you: and ye shall be hated of all nations for my name's sake.

And then shall many be offended, and shall betray one another, and shall hate one another.

And many false prophets shall rise, and shall deceive many.

And because iniquity shall abound, the love of many shall wax cold.

But he that shall endure unto the end, the same shall be saved.

And this gospel of the kingdom shall be preached in all the world for a witness unto all nations; and then shall the end come.

Matthew 24:8-14

The second question the disciples asked Jesus was, "What shall be the sign of Thy coming?" In this passage is His answer to them. He said, "I'll tell you what it will be. Nation will rise against nation." So when you're gone (did you notice I said you?), then nation will rise against nation, kingdom against kingdom, there will be famines, pestilence, earthquakes in various places, which are already happening. And He said,

"These are the beginning of sorrows." In other words, this is the beginning of the Tribulation.

What are they going to do to Christians? They're going to deliver them up as though they are criminals; they're even going to kill some of them. Believers are going to be hated by all nations. All this will cause some people to become cold to the things of God because the pressure will be so bad. There again will be that old, dumb false prophet, that deceptive, seducing spirit, in that Satan will have false religions and all kinds of deceptions. But look at what verse 13 says: "But he that shall endure unto the end, the same shall be saved."

That doesn't have to do with eternal life because the Bible says that when you're saved, when you receive Jesus, you have eternal life. At any instance you die, if you have Jesus in your heart, you're going to go to heaven.* But these are people who either get saved in this hard time of the Tribulation or they come back to God. So it's going to be a heavy-duty time filled with pressure and persecution.

But He said that if they would hold on and not give up and not get cold in their love for God, some way God will come on the scene and save them out of the situation. He'll find a way to get them through it.

Jesus' answer to the disciples' question is not all bad news; there's some very good news here. During the Tribulation, the Gospel will be preached. Revelation points to that fact. The reason is that God loves people, and He's trying to get people to come to Him. (Later on, we will see how much He

---

* If you have never accepted Jesus as your Savior and would like to, there's a prayer you can pray at the end of this book.

loves Muslims, how much He loves the Persian Empire, the Elamites, and His plans for getting them.)

In verse 14 He says that the Gospel will be preached in all the world as a witness to all the nations, and then the end will come. You may wonder how they can preach it when there will be so much persecution. We've got so many ways to preach the Gospel now—e-mail, Web sites, twenty-four-hour-a-day TV broadcasts to name a few. You can't keep the good news out anymore. God has many ways to get the Gospel preached and get it where He wants it to go.

The world is looking to the church. This is our moment; this is our hour. We're the pretribulation saints. We need to be out there shaking the bushes, rattling their cages, and telling them that Jesus is coming, and they need to be sure that they have Him in their hearts.

This will be a dark, heavy, hard, difficult time. The Gospel will be preached everywhere, but there will be deception, Christians being persecuted, people holding on, the love of many waxing cold, a lot of false cults—but that's what Jesus told us to expect in His answer to "What will be the sign of Thy coming?"

GREAT PERSECUTION

"Therefore when you see the 'abomination of desolation,' spoken of by Daniel the prophet, standing in the holy place" (whoever reads, let him understand),

"then let those who are in Judea flee to the mountains.

"Let him who is on the housetop not go down to take anything out of his house.

"And let him who is in the field not go back to get his clothes.

"But woe to those who are pregnant and to those who are nursing babies in those days!

"And pray that your flight may not be in winter or on the Sabbath.

"For then there will be great tribulation, such as has not been since the beginning of the world until this time, no, nor ever shall be.

"And unless those days were shortened, no flesh would be saved; but for the elect's sake those days will be shortened.

"Then if anyone says to you, 'Look, here is the Christ!' or 'There!' do not believe it.

"For false christs and false prophets will rise and show great signs and wonders to deceive, if possible, even the elect.

"See, I have told you beforehand.

"Therefore if they say to you, 'Look, He is in the desert!' do not go out; or 'Look, He is in the inner rooms!' do not believe it.

"For as the lightning comes from the east and flashes to the west, so also will the coming of the Son of Man be."
Matthew 24:15-27 NKJV

The term *abomination of desolation* doesn't really mean much to most Christians. We say, "Oh yes, it's in the book of

Daniel and in Matthew 24," but many don't know what it is. The abomination of desolation has to do with the Jews. This is the answer to the disciples' last question, "What will be the sign of the end of the age?" There will be an abomination of desolation.

We will see more on this later, but it will be an idol of the Antichrist set up in the temple in the Holy of Holies. How are the Jews connected with that? Verse 16 tells us that it will take place in Judea, which is where the Jews live. Then in verses 22 and 24 when Jesus spoke of the elect, He was referring to the Jews because the Bible always calls the Jews the elect. So all of this passage has to do with the Jews and the horrible persecution that will come upon them, especially those who have received Jesus, because they turn against the Antichrist.

Of course, we see the deception in this same thing. There's deception for pretribulation Christians, there's deception for nations, and there's deception for Jews. The devil is always out there trying to get people off the truth.

That's why it's so important to teach our children the truth. We need to take preventative measures. It's hard to get people out of false doctrine. You have to work hard and get them in the Word. Why not teach them the truth before they get into deception? We can prevent that. We can give our children a good foundation by getting them in the Bible at an early age. Then when the junk comes along, they will be able to say, "That's not true. That's not in the Bible."

In Matthew 24:27 the Bible tells us what happens at the end of the age: Jesus is coming.

For as the lightning cometh out of the east, and shineth even unto the west; so shall also the coming of the Son of man be.

Before that happens, the Jews will see a "little" Rapture during this time. It doesn't tell us here, but it tells us in Revelation 11 that there will be two witnesses who will preach to the Jews during the hard part of the Tribulation.

These two witnesses will be sent by God. They will be strong and powerful, and they will really preach the Word. The Antichrist will eventually have them killed, but after three and a half days of their bodies being left in the street for the whole world to see, all at once, they will come alive again and go up—thus, another Rapture.

Why is that so important to the Jews? I believe it is because the two witnesses are their two favorite prophets whom they love—Moses and Elijah. To see these two men come and preach and die and go up is a powerful witness to them, because the Jews never believed that Jesus was really raised from the dead. They said that somebody stole His body. But when their two prophets preach Jesus, die, and are raised from the dead right before their eyes, the Jews will get on board. So there will be tremendous signs to the Jewish people about who Jesus is in this time.

After these signs happen, Jesus is going to come again. So, there will be a Rapture at this time of the church that was saved or came back to God and of the Jewish believers. But are you in this one? No, because you'll already be up there!

A GATHERING OF EAGLES

"For wherever the carcass is, there the eagles will be gathered together.

"Immediately after the tribulation of those days the sun will be darkened, and the moon will not give its light; the stars will fall from heaven, and the powers of the heavens will be shaken.

"Then the sign of the Son of Man will appear in heaven, and then all the tribes of the earth will mourn, and they will see the Son of Man coming on the clouds of heaven with power and great glory.

"And He will send His angels with a great sound of a trumpet, and they will gather together His elect from the four winds, from one end of heaven to the other.

"Now learn this parable from the fig tree: When its branch has already become tender and puts forth leaves, you know that summer is near.

"So you also, when you see all these things, know that it is near—at the doors!

"Assuredly, I say to you, this generation will by no means pass away till all these things take place.

"Heaven and earth will pass away, but My words will by no means pass away."

Matthew 24:28-35 NKJV

We saw that verse 27 talks of the coming of Jesus. When He comes, He's going to establish His kingdom on the earth.

This passage gives a description of what's going to happen, but not chronologically.

Verse 28, which talks about the eagles gathering together around the carcass, has bothered me for years. What's the carcass? Who are the eagles? Some translations say vultures (I believe incorrectly). This has to do with a Rapture, and the eagles are gathered around a carcass? This doesn't fit in with the rest of it.

Eagles don't eat meat; vultures do. So what are these eagles doing around a dead body? The key words here are "dead body," because the eagles will be gathered around the Lamb who was "slain from the foundation of the world" (Rev. 13:8). In other words, all the Christians are going to gather around Jesus.

Wasn't Jesus slain and then arose from the dead? Did Buddha die and rise from the dead? Did Mohammed die and rise from the dead? Did the over three hundred thousand idols of Hindus die and rise from the dead? No, but Jesus died, because if He didn't die for our sins, there's no hope for us. Did He arise from the dead? We're going to gather around the slain, resurrected Christ, because if He didn't die, there is no resurrection power. So He had to die for our sins.

Now look at Revelation 5:6.

> And I beheld, and, lo, in the midst of the throne and of the four beasts, and in the midst of the elders, stood a Lamb as it had been slain, having seven horns and seven eyes, which are the seven Spirits of God sent forth into all the earth.

We are going to be so excited to see Jesus because we know that He loved us so much that He died for us. That's what the followers of false religion can't get. They don't understand the tremendous love of God, the love of Jesus, and the love of the Holy Spirit for us, that God (in the form of His Son Jesus) would literally die for us because He loved us. So the eagles will be gathered around Him.

Then Jesus says something in Matthew 24:34 that is so key for us. He says, "...this generation will by no means pass away till all these things take place." That is scary. The Tribulation is seven years, and we are in pretribulation days. According to the Bible, you and I are in this generation. God put us here now because He loves us and wants to use us. He has a wonderful destiny and a sovereign plan for every one of us.

The last verse in this passage says, "Heaven and earth will pass away, but My words will by no means pass away." Where are you going to put your confidence? Are you going to put your confidence in the newspapers and what they say? Are you going to put your confidence in magazines? Or can you trust God's Word? Is He a holy God? Does His Word have integrity? Can you believe in God's Word? Yes, you can.

That is where we must live and that is where our focus must be. We've got to keep our focus on Jesus, the One who died and rose from the dead. We've got to keep our focus on His Word. We've got to be very serious about our walk with God in this time. This is no time to play around.

You may say, "Well, I'm not perfect. What if He comes and I didn't read my Bible that day?" I don't believe Jesus is coming for perfect people. I believe that He's coming for people who are looking for Him and have their focus on Him and have kept their passion for Him.

Remember, we're not talking about ritual; we're talking about relationship. So if you haven't read your Bible that day, but you're living for Jesus, if He's the passion of your heart, you're going to make it in the first Rapture. If you yelled at your husband or your wife right before Jesus appears, I believe you're going to make it. If you kicked the dog or if you snapped at somebody, I believe you're going to make it because Jesus is the center of your heart.

CHAPTER 3

GOD'S PLAN FOR MUSLIMS

Muslims make up one-fifth of the world's population. There are over a billion people that claim the Islamic faith. Does God not care about those people? What is His promise for them for the end times? Does He not want them to come into the kingdom and make the first Rapture too? Because we've been attacked by some of them so badly, what are we to be like with them? What is our place? What is the attitude towards them that we need to take as the church?

In this chapter, we're going to be looking at the Islamic world and what God has to say about the Muslims, and how they relate to us. I think you'll be really excited when you see God's plan regarding all this.

When we look at the Islamic world, we have to look at their holy book, because that's the core of their belief. The core of our belief is our Bible; we always go to the Bible totally. This is God's Word. This is where we live. This is our heart. This is our passion. When we have a problem, this is our plumbline.

The Koran is the holy book of the Islamic faith. I think that the major thing about it that would make you and me hurt for their people is the fact that the word *love* is never mentioned in the Koran.

Can you imagine worshiping a god who doesn't love you? There is no word for *love* in their Koran. But when we read our holy book, from Genesis to Revelation, it says God loves us. In fact, God loves us so much that He sent His Son to die for us. The Bible tells us that we are to abide in His love. (John 15:10.) And He is constantly sending a love message to us—His correction, His training, His rebuking of us in love, His encouraging us in love. It is so sweet that we have a loving Father who will do that to us.

Another thing that we find about the Koran is that it talks about worshiping Allah, which is actually a name of a heathen idol. In the time of Mohammed, around the seventh century, they had three hundred and sixty days to a year, and they had a different idol that they worshiped for each day. The one they considered the greatest idol that had the most strength, the most power, was the moon god, and Allah refers to the moon god.

If you notice also on all mosques, they have the crescent, which is the symbol of the moon that goes back to their worshiping of the moon god. So when people say to you, "Whether we worship Allah or some other god, we're all worshiping the same god; we're all on the same path, but we just take a few different ways to that god," that is not true. I don't worship a moon god. Every month there's a beautiful full moon, but I worship the God who made the moon.

There is one God, there is one Savior, there is one Holy Spirit, and there is one book of truth, which is the Word of God. But we can see in the Bible and throughout history many false religions coming up making a way for the greatest false religion of all, which will be when the Antichrist raises himself up and puts himself as an idol in the temple.

False religion can be dangerous. How tragic that over three hundred times Muslims are told to kill Christians and Jews in the Koran (fortunately not all Muslims go along with this). So when you look at the heart of their holy book, you can understand some of the Islamic radicals taking it and doing what it says. If you can understand that, then you can see where it is coming from.

These radicals are certainly our enemies, and there is no question we've been terribly attacked by them. But look at what Matthew 5:44 says.

> But I say unto you, Love your enemies, bless them that curse you, do good to them that hate you, and pray for them which despitefully use you, and persecute you.

According to this verse, we are supposed to love our enemies and pray for them, praying what God says in His Word.

There is no question that we are at the end of time, but what an awesome time to be born because we can bring light in darkness, and we can pray and change things. We can love where there is hatred involved.

To find out where it all began, we're going to go way back to the book of Genesis, where we will see the beginning of the Persian Empire and of all the roots of the Islamic people.

ISLAMIC ORIGIN

The children of Shem; Elam, and Asshur, and Arphaxad, and Lud, and Aram.

Genesis 10:22

Shem is one of the sons of Noah, and this is the son that the Jewish people come from. Shem had five sons. Elam, his first son, is important because the Elamites are the Persians and that part of the Arab world. Now Persians are not Arabs, but they are Islamic in their religion, and, basically, they are related. So if we look at Elam, we would say that he's related to the Jewish people.

We're going to see that God loved Elam; He loved the five sons of Shem. In fact, He said that Shem would be the one son who would bring the revelation of God to the whole world.[1] We're descendants of Jephthah, and we know that Indo-Europeans are descendants of Jephthah and that the descendants of Ham are primarily African. But Shem has to do with the Arab, Persian, Jewish people. So they are connected; they're in the same family.

Genesis 11: 10 says, "These are the generations of Shem: Shem was an hundred years old, and begat Arphaxad two years after the flood." Arphaxad is important to us because Abraham came from him. We won't refer a lot to Arphaxad, but let's look at Abraham for a moment.

Abraham lived up in that area, in Ur, where the people worshiped the moon. God called Abraham out of idolatry and separated him, and the Bible says that he became God's friend and a great man of faith. (James 2:23.) God always gets a lot of mileage out of everything He does; I always say that He is so economical. He certainly gets a lot of mileage out of calling Abraham, who demonstrated what it is to have a faith walk.

In Genesis 14 we see the first terrorist and the first recorded war and how Abraham was involved.

> And it came to pass in the days of Amraphel king of Shinar, Arioch king of Ellasar, Chedorlaomer king of Elam, and Tidal king of nations;
>
> That these made war with Bera king of Sodom, and with Birsha king of Gomorrah, Shinab king of Admah, and Shemeber king of Zeboiim, and the king of Bela, which is Zoar.
>
> All these were joined together in the vale of Siddim, which is the salt sea.
>
> Genesis 14:1-3

The Elamites were involved in this war. They came down to fight against Sodom and Gomorrah. Five kings got together, but the Elamites attacked them, taking all the people of Sodom and Gomorrah captive (including Abraham's nephew Lot who lived in Sodom) and taking all the wealth. Soon Abraham heard about it.

Now Abraham knew about these people. Remember, he lived among them. He knew what the moon god was. He knew the way they lived. But he had the living God. The story in Genesis tells how he took all three hundred and fourteen of his servants and went up and attacked these five kings and won! He took back the wealth, brought back Lot, and restored the wealth to Sodom and Gomorrah. It is in that time that he met Melchizedek, a priest of God.[2]

Do you think it was a witness to those five kings that Abraham worshiped the living God, that his God gave him the victory and made his three hundred and fourteen servants greater than five armies of five nations? Yes, they rescued Lot. Yes, Abraham met Melchizedek. Yes, Abraham and his people belonged to God. But God wanted the people who were destroyed here too, the ones who had been the destroyers.

Does God love people? Does God love the Muslims? Absolutely He loves them. Does He want to reach them? Yes! Does He want one billion people to go to hell? Absolutely not, so He had a plan that was a witness to them.

BABYLON FALLS

When Nebuchadnezzar captured Judea, Daniel was taken captive along with many other key young men out of Judah. (Dan. 1:3,6.) In the captivity, Nebuchadnezzar was the king of Babylon, which again would be in the part of the world that spread across Iran, Iraq, and Pakistan. It was a huge empire at that time. When they reached Babylon, they found that Nebuchadnezzar worshiped idols. But the three Hebrew children (Shadrach, Meshach, and Abednego) and Daniel made a real commitment that they were only going to worship the living God. In doing so, they became a very strong witness to this empire.

Then one night Nebuchadnezzar had a dream. (Dan. 2:1.) He dreamed of four major national entities, which are very key because they're really part of the history of the world and its relationship to Israel. Later on we'll look at this in depth, but in His dream, he dreamed of a creature that has a head of gold, arms of silver, and a stomach of brass. It has legs of iron and feet of iron and clay. When he woke up, he couldn't remember the dream, but he knew that it was important.

All his magicians, astrologers, and sorcerers couldn't tell him the dream or what it meant, so eventually they called in Daniel. He was given the dream and the interpretation from God; then he told the king the dream and what the revelation was: "You're the head of gold. But the next empire that's going to overcome you will be the Medes and the Persians, and they will have a very strong empire."

The remnants of the Persian Empire are still around today, and most fascinating, Iran, Iraq, and Pakistan are definitely from the Persian Empire. So this was a witness of God to those people, saying that He cared about the Medes and the Persians.

Then in Daniel 7:5, we see again the Medes and the Persians who are involved in end-time prophecy. Remember, God loves Muslims and He has a plan to get to them. He's not thinking, *I love them, but I don't really want to be bothered with them. I've got to get the Jews and the Gentiles in.* No, God has a plan for all people. He's knocking at the door of their hearts all the time. We're seeing how He was knocking at the door of the Muslims.

Babylon came to a peak and then it fell, and Nebuchadnezzar received the Lord; he actually became a believer. Daniel 4 gives his personal testimony of this happening. But after Nebuchadnezzar died, his grandson took the throne. His name was Belshazzar, and he was very ungodly, very idolatrous.

One night, he had a big party, and he called for the implements that his grandfather took in captivity from the temple
of Jerusalem. He said, "Bring up the gold goblets and bring
up the silver goblets that were used in the temple to worship
their God. We're going to drink wine from them and worship
the gods of wood and silver and stone and earth" (Dan. 5:3,4).

When he said that, the Bible tells how a hand suddenly
appeared and wrote something on the wall. Would you say
that this is a rather strong witness? The hand wrote, "Mene,
Mene, Tekel, upharsin," and we know that Daniel came up
and interpreted it, saying, "Your kingdom is weighed and
found wanting. And tonight it will be divided to the Medes
and the Persians" (vv. 27,28, author paraphrase). That was a
true dream that Nebuchadnezzar had, and it was a witness to
these people.

Nobody could take over Babylon. The walls were so high
and so wide; it is said that they could drive thirteen chariots
abreast around the walls of Babylon. But history tells us how
the Medes and the Persians took over the city that night.

There was a river that went through Babylon, the Euphrates River. So the Medes and the Persians very coolly changed
the course of that river, and they began to dig little causeways
and the water began to go down. Of course, Belshazzar was
having a big party in Babylon, and no one realized that the
water was going down under the gate.

Meanwhile, the Medes and the Persians waited for that
water to go down low enough to swim under the gate. And
that night they took the city and totally conquered the Babylonian Empire.

You may wonder, *What does that have to do with Muslims?* It has everything to do with them. This is their roots, and God loves them and wants to minister to these people. These are the descendants of Shem. They are the relatives of the Jewish people.

CYRUS PRENAMED

Now in the first year of Cyrus king of Persia, that the word of the Lord by the mouth of Jeremiah might be fulfilled, the Lord stirred up the spirit of Cyrus king of Persia, that he made a proclamation throughout all his kingdom, and put it also in writing, saying,

Thus saith Cyrus king of Persia, The Lord God of heaven hath given me all the kingdoms of the earth; and he hath charged me to build him an house at Jerusalem, which is in Judah.

Ezra 1:1,2

Cyrus was the king of the Medes and the Persians, and he said, "God told me I'm to build His temple for Him." Why would He do that? If you look at Isaiah 45, you'll see that God prophesied Cyrus's name over a hundred years before he was born. Now is God awesome? Is He Jehovah-Jireh ("The Lord Will Provide")?[3] He said, "I've got people who are in captivity living down there in Babylon, and after seventy years, I want them to go back to Jerusalem. So I'm going to raise up a man named Cyrus who will conquer Babylon, and he'll let My people go back." Let's read about him in Isaiah 45:1-4.

Thus saith the Lord to his anointed, to Cyrus, whose right hand I have holden, to subdue nations before him; and I will loose the loins of kings, to open before him the two leaved gates; and the gates shall not be shut [describing Babylon];

I will go before thee, and make the crooked places straight: I will break in pieces the gates of brass, and cut in sunder the bars of iron.

(These gates had not been built yet, but God said they would be of brass. That was the exact description of the gates of Babylon before they were built.)

And I will give thee the treasures of darkness, and hidden riches of secret places, that thou mayest know that I, the Lord, which call thee by thy name, am the God of Israel.

For Jacob my servant's sake, and Israel mine elect, I have even called thee by thy name: I have surnamed thee, though thou hast not known me.

I can imagine somebody going up to Cyrus one day and saying, "Cyrus, did you know that your name is in the Bible? It's in the book of Isaiah. And God says about you that He prenamed you before you were ever born and that He gave you Babylon. He opened those big brass gates. He opened those bars of iron, but He did it for a purpose. You're to let God's people go back and rebuild their temple."

This news probably stunned Cyrus at first. Then he must have thought, *I better do it*. Was that a revelation to the Persian Empire about a living God, that He would prename their number one king? Does God care about these people? Does He want to get to them? Absolutely!

GOD'S WAY OF WITNESSING

The book of Ezra tells of another Persian king named Darius. When the Israelites came back to rebuild the temple, the local residents who lived there were not happy about it. They said, "No, you can't rebuild the temple," and they came out and attacked them. They even wrote a letter to the Persian Empire, saying, "Make them stop." Is it any wonder that the Israelites got discouraged and stopped rebuilding for a while?

Then two prophets in Jerusalem and Judah named Haggai and Zechariah rose up and began to prophesy to them, and it stirred up the people to finish the temple. (Ezra 5:1.) But when they started working on the temple, the local residents came out against them again and said, "You can't do that. The Persian Empire said you can't." But the Israelites answered, "We're going to do it anyway because Cyrus told us we could, and we're going to finish it." They said, "Well, Cyrus is dead, and you're not going to finish it," and the Israelites replied, "Just try and stop us."

The governors and other officials allowed them to keep rebuilding the temple, while they sent a letter to Darius, who was the new Persian king. They wrote, "The Israelites insist that King Cyrus of Babylon signed a decree saying that they could build this temple, and they say that they're going to finish it. Please check into this and let us know what you decide on the matter." (vv. 5-17.)

Darius checked everything out and found that they were right: Cyrus had not only signed a decree, but he had sent them the money to finish the temple.

God is so good. He is for His people, but that was also a witness to Darius and a witness to the Persian Empire. Do you think Daniel was a witness? Do you think these kings were not witnesses? Somebody was prenamed in the Bible, because God loves the Elamites and the Persians.

WITNESS OF A BEAUTY QUEEN

One of the most outstanding examples of someone who was a witness to these people is Queen Esther, who got into the Persian Empire through a beauty contest. You may not have known that they had beauty contests in the Bible, but if you remember, the Persian King Ahasuerus became very unhappy with Queen Vashti. He had thrown a big, lavish feast at the palace in which they ate and drank for months, and the king brought out all the beautiful women. But he felt that his wife, Vashti, was the most beautiful woman of all, so he called for her to come out naked.[4] Well, the idea disgusted her, and she said, "Forget it, I'm not doing that," which made him really angry at her. (Est. 1:10-12.)

Then his counselor said, "If you let her get away with this, every woman will start acting the same way and disobey their husbands. They'll stop cooking for their husbands and start acting ugly. You better divorce her and get her out, because that's going to be the worst example in the world to the other women." But God used this, because God is economical and

48

He loves His people. Yes, He loves the Jews, but He loves these people too. He loves the Elamites.

What did God do? Well, the king was looking for a beautiful young woman to be his new queen, and who showed up but Esther. She was not a Mede or a Persian; no one in the king's court knew that she was a Jewish believer, and she came in and was made the new queen. (Est. 2:17,20.)

Soon the Jews fell on hard times. In the king's court, there was a very wicked man named Haman, and he got the king to sign a decree to have a holocaust and kill all the Jews. (Est. 3:8-11.) We may be in a hard time, too, but God will win, just as He won for Esther and the Jewish people. If we will stay focused on God and pray, He will win over all the situations in our nation and in our lives. It's a key time for us, as it was for Esther.

When she found out about the decree, she and Mordecai began to fast and pray, and she got her maids and he got the Jewish people fasting and praying. Soon God gave her a plan that would cause her to win the king's heart.

They say the way to a man's heart is through his stomach, and Esther tried it. She could have had a nervous breakdown and said, "Oh, you're going to kill all my people!" But instead, she invited her husband to dinner. Well, the king was so taken with Esther and her feast that he said, "What do you want? I'm so impressed. This is such a good dinner." She said, "I just want you to come back again," and she added, "Be sure you bring Haman." (Est. 5:8.)

The king and Haman came for dinner the next night and the king was so pleased that he asked her again, "Esther, what do you want?" Her answer startled him, "I want my people." He asked her, "Who are your people?" and she said, "The Jewish people, and you've signed a decree for them all to be killed."

The king was so angry with Haman over this that he ordered Haman hanged and a second decree written, saying that the Jews could defend themselves against anyone who attacked them. So no one came against them for fear of what the Jews would do to them. (Est. 9:2.)

Esther stepped in and saved the Jewish people, and that was a witness to the Persian Empire. It wasn't a witness just to the Jewish people. It's not just a witness to you and me. It is a witness that God loved the Persian Empire. He loved the Elamites; He wanted to get them into the kingdom too.

GOD WANTS MUSLIMS

When I was memorizing John 8, the Holy Spirit spoke to me of His love for all people. That chapter tells about the woman who was taken in the act of adultery. The men who caught her brought her before the Lord and asked Him, "Should we stone her?" Then Jesus stooped down and wrote on the ground. Finally, He stood up and said, "...He who is without sin among you, let him throw a stone at her first," and they all walked away. The woman was left there alone, and they didn't stone her. Jesus told her that He didn't condemn her and to "...go and sin no more." Then He said, "...I am the light of the world...."

When I read that, I thought, *Oh, that is so good. No matter how dark the sin, Jesus will be the light. His Light is greater than the darkness of any sin.*

Just then the Holy Spirit said to me, *You rejoice because she was set free, but I grieve over the ones I lost.* Surprised, I asked, "Who did You lose?" and He said, *Her accusers. I gave more attention to her accusers than I did to her because I wanted them as much as I wanted her.*

Oh, I thought, *God, You want Muslims as much as You want anybody else!* That is so true because God loves all people, as evidenced by what He was doing all the time in that chapter—He was being a witness to them.

One of the major themes we see throughout the Bible is that God loves these people. From Genesis all the way into the New Testament, God was witnessing to them—and He is still witnessing.

WITNESS OF THE WISE MEN

Now when Jesus was born in Bethlehem of Judaea in the days of Herod the king, behold, there came wise men from the east to Jerusalem,

Saying, Where is he that is born King of the Jews? for we have seen his star in the east, and are come to worship him.
Matthew 2:1,2

In this account of the wise men who came to Jesus, it said that they had seen the star for two years and had come to Jerusalem from the east, which would have been Iran, Iraq, and the Persian Empire. The wise men were very much into the study of stars. It was known that there was a prophesied star, and people had been waiting for that star for centuries. The above passage tells the purpose of the star.

When I get into the Scriptures and dig into them, I often think, *God, I love the Bible more every day.* The integrity of God's Word is undeniable. We see that when He prophesied about the star way back in the Pentateuch in Numbers 24:17. Of all people to prophesy, it was Balaam. He possessed a gift of prophecy and was called upon by a Moabite king named Balak to curse the Israelites before they could enter the land of Canaan. On the way there, God impressed upon Balaam, through an unusual incident with his donkey and an encounter with the angel of the Lord, that he should only say what God would tell him to say.

God wouldn't let him curse His people but only bless them, and he said, "I shall see Him, but not now. I shall behold Him, but not nigh: there shall come a Star out of Jacob, and a Scepter shall arise out of Israel, and shall smite the corners of Moab, and destroy all the children of Sheth."

Notice the wise men said something similar: "There's arisen a star, and this star is going to lead us to a king." They had been watching for that star a long time, as did many others. Century after century, people who study the stars wondered, "Where is that star of Jacob that's going to lead us to the king?" until finally the star appeared. It appeared for two years evidently over the area of Iran and Iraq, wherever the wise men were.

When the star began to move, they followed the star, and it led them to the King of kings and Lord of lords—Jesus. Who is God going to lead the Muslims to? Jesus—He is the Star. In following the star, the wise men were a witness to the Persian Empire about Jesus Christ, the Son of God, His Scepter.

THE CHURCH AT BABYLON

What God did at Pentecost, when all those in the Upper Room began speaking "...with other tongues, as the Spirit gave them utterance" (Acts 2:4), is so key to this message.

> **And they were all amazed and marvelled, saying one to another, Behold, are not all these which speak Galilaeans?**
>
> **And how hear we every man in our own tongue, wherein we were born?**
>
> **Parthians, and Medes, and Elamites, and the dwellers in Mesopotamia, and in Judaea, and Cappadocia, in Pontus, and Asia.**
>
> Acts 2:7-9

Were Elamites present on the day of Pentecost? Did they know about the star? Did they know about Jesus? Did they know about the outpouring of the Holy Spirit? God loved them enough to get them there, to tell them about it for centuries and lead them to the King of kings. He had a crowd of them there on the day of Pentecost. When the disciples spoke in tongues, the Elamites heard their own language being spoken.

The Persians today speak Farsi. I don't know if they spoke Farsi back then, but undoubtedly at Pentecost somebody spoke in tongues in the Persian language of that day, and it must have sounded like Farsi. We know what they said. The Bible says that they told of the wonderful works of God and that the Persians heard them because God loves these people, and in every way, He's giving a witness to them that He loves them.

In 1 Peter 5:13, Peter wrote to the church at Babylon and said, "The church that is at Babylon, elected together with you, saluteth you; and so doth Marcus my son." What happened? Out of Pentecost, out of this star coming and guiding the wise men to Jesus the King of kings, a church rose up in Babylon, maybe even where Saddam Hussein lived. But they had churches up among the Elamites back then because God loved them. There was a tremendous witness of God and of His love to them, and they came into the kingdom.

TURNED BACK TO GOD

These areas of the world were very strong in Christianity until the seventh century, when Mohammed arose and wrote the Koran. I haven't read the whole book through, although I've read quite a bit of it. We've seen some things that it talks about. Women are another subject. The Koran discusses a man's responsibility to beat his wife and correct her rebellious behavior. It also says that the only way a woman can go to heaven is if her husband lets her.

Something else in the Koran is that Ishmael is the seed of promise, not Isaac. That means that two thousand years or more before he came on the scene, God was saying Isaac was the seed of promise. Now suddenly God changed His mind twenty-five hundred years later and said, "Oops, I made a mistake, not Isaac, but Ishmael." So Mohammed rewrote all of it to say that it's the Islamic people who have the promise, not the people who have Jesus.

God is love, and God so loved the world and He came on the scene, but the Koran says that He didn't come in with a message to convert people. He came in with a sword and said, "Either you believe in Mohammed or you're dead." They also say that Jesus is a prophet. In fact, they believe in six major prophets, but Mohammed is the main prophet because he's the last one, and he wrote the last revelation, which is the Koran.

Many people were killed or brought into the Islamic religion. I'm not even going to call it a faith because there's not much faith to it. How sad that it came out of a Christian empire. It makes you want to spit at the devil because he's the one who's behind it.

But there is good news out of this. Look at the next two Scriptures:

> And it shall come to pass in that day, that the Lord shall set his hand again the second time to recover the remnant of his people, which shall be left, from Assyria, and from Egypt, and from Pathros, and from Cush, and from Elam, and from Shinar, and from Hamath, and from the islands of the sea.
>
> Isaiah 11:11

Elam and Shinar are Babylon, and God is saying, "I'm going to recover a remnant of people, and they're going to come out of Elam."

Then in Jeremiah 49:39 God promises that He wants to do something to get His people.

> But it shall come to pass in the latter days, that I will bring again the captivity of Elam, saith the Lord.

In this verse God is saying that He's going to turn this whole thing around and turn the Elamites back to Him. I believe that in these last days God is doing something that will include a great revival in the Islamic world. In Nebuchadnezzar's dream he saw the head of gold. He saw the arms of silver, representing the Medes and the Persians. He saw the belly and thighs of brass, representing the Greeks. He saw the legs of iron. He saw the toes of iron and clay, and he saw those four major empires that would be upon the earth.

But then he saw something else. He saw a rock, and this rock came out of heaven and smashed the whole thing, all of these empires. This rock kept getting bigger and bigger until it filled all the earth. Who is this rock? It is the Rock of Ages, Jesus Christ, and He will fill the whole earth, as the Word said, with His glory and knowledge. (Isa. 6:3; 11:9.)

I believe that there's a great time of revival coming into the Islamic world. As watchers, we can help pray it in.

SECTION 2

REVELATION
REVEALED

CHAPTER 4

THE "HOUSE" OF REVELATION

The last book of the Bible—Revelation—is packed with endtime truths that are so important to our time. As you look ahead in Revelation, you will realize God's provision for the future for His children and find that the mysteries surrounding the second coming of the Lord are revealed. To make God's miracle plan easier for you to understand, I'm going to present an overview of Revelation in this chapter. Later on, I will bring it to life in a more in-depth study.

Revelation can be best understood by dividing it into sections. To help people grasp the message, I like to use the illustration of a seven-room home (see Figure 4.1). Moving from left to right, the advancement through this "house" represents the progression through the Revelation timeline.

Notice the passageways, or "doors," which lead from room to room. You can see that the second room is unique in that it leads three ways—to the third, fourth, and fifth rooms. Although the timeline itself moves from left to right, rooms three, four, and five represent a single time frame seen from a variety of perspectives. This will make more sense as we walk together through this "home."

THE STRUCTURE OF REVELATION

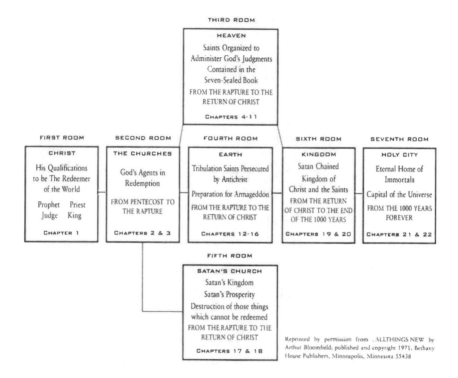

FIRST ROOM

The first section of Revelation (Chapter 1) presents a powerful fourfold description of our Redeemer. It is a beautiful and highly symbolic picture of Jesus Christ as Prophet, Priest, Judge, and King. These four aspects of our Savior reappear throughout the remainder of the book. We can see that Jesus is well qualified to be the Savior of the world.

From this room there is only one door leading to the second room.

SECOND ROOM

Entering into the second room, we find the second section of Revelation (Chapters 2 and 3), which refers primarily to the church and to church history, from the Day of Pentecost through the Rapture.

The church is God's agent in redemption, the body of Christ in the earth. I personally believe that the local churches pictured (Ephesus, Thyatira, Laodicea, etc.) represent churches that actually existed at the time—and in a broader sense, illustrate seven ages of church history.

As already mentioned, this second room offers three doors through which to pass to the events of rooms three, four, and five (see Figure 4.1). Events in these three rooms occur simultaneously, and cover the period from the Rapture to the Return of Christ. Although they cover the same time span, the three rooms present three different viewpoints.

The third room portrays events chronologically from heaven's point of view. The fourth describes events in topical order from the perspective of the earth. The fifth room shows the same period of time from Satan's position. Remembering that will help you avoid much confusion as we continue our "walk."

THIRD ROOM

The third room begins in Revelation 4. The church ages are over and we see the activities in heaven immediately after the

Rapture. Plus, we will see events on earth, but from a heavenly perspective (in Chapters 4-11).

This section contains John's vision of God's throne, the seven-sealed book, and the seven trumpet judgments. Keep in mind that this section covers the time from the Rapture until Christ's return with the saints (us!) to destroy the wicked kings of the earth at Armageddon.

From the third room, we see a door leading into the sixth room (see Figure 4.1). But first, let's study the fourth and fifth rooms, which cover the same timeframe as the third.

FOURTH ROOM

Another door from the second room opens into the fourth section. Like the third, this fourth room begins with the Rapture and ends with the return of Christ. It pictures events on earth, showing the Antichrist and those who are left behind on earth at that time. This fourth section is comprised of Revelation, Chapters 12-16, which provide a second witness to Chapters 4-11. We will soon see that Chapters 17 and 18 comprise a third witness.

Symbolic language is used extensively in these chapters. From this room we look down on the earth and witness the activities resulting from the happenings in heaven. Later, the point of view changes, and we are on the earth to witness the man-child caught up to heaven. Then we see the persecution of the Antichrist and the conflict of the armies of the world against the Lord. (Remember, later on we will study all this in-depth.)

As the third room did, the fourth room leads to room six (see Figure 4.1), but first we need to see what happens in the fifth room.

FIFTH ROOM

Do you recall that there are three doors in the second room? The last of those three doors opens downward to the fifth room (Chapters 17 and 18). This "room" follows the activities of the false church of Satan, pictured as the harlot of Revelation (in Chapter 17).[1] She is the counterfeit of the true church, which is represented by the woman in Chapter 12. The true church will enter the New Jerusalem and make it home for all eternity, while the church of Satan will go into perdition.

This fifth room provides additional details to the events of rooms three and four. Here we see the mystery of evil and its final destruction. There is no outlet from this section, because everything that cannot be redeemed will be destroyed.

SIXTH ROOM

The sixth room (Chapters 19 and 20) describes the kingdom age. After seven years of tribulation, Jesus is crowned King of kings and Lord of lords, followed by the great wedding in heaven, the marriage supper of the Lamb. We are united as the bride of Christ and reign with Him during the Millennium and forever.

The Millennium, during which Satan is bound in chains, is a time of preparation for the earth to be turned over to God. At the end of this thousand-year period, Satan prepares for a final battle. Fire from heaven devours his followers. Ultimately, Satan is cast into the lake of fire.[2]

From this room only one door leads us into the final room.

SEVENTH ROOM

The seventh room (Chapters 21 and 22) ushers us into the very presence of God, the eternal home of the saints. As the apostle Paul said, "...Eye hath not seen, nor ear heard, neither have entered into the heart of man" all the wonderful things that God has for us in that day (1 Cor. 2:9).

You may have noticed that there are no other doors leading off from this room. The reason is that this is both the end of the house and of time (as we know it). We will be so overjoyed with God's plans for eternity that we will never even consider leaving this "room."

THE WRAP-UP OF "HIS-STORY"

It could be said that Revelation is the wrap-up of His-story, referring to Jesus. In Revelation 22:13 Jesus said, "I am Alpha and Omega, the beginning and the end, the first and the last." That is so obvious as we look at another aspect of the books of Genesis and Revelation. Genesis has been called the seed plot of the Bible because it is the book of beginnings, and Revelation is a book of endings.

Genesis begins this story with four prophecies of Jesus. Jesus, our Savior, fulfills all these prophecies in Revelation. He truly is the mark of history.

FIRST PROPHECY

The first prophecy of Jesus in the book of Genesis foretells that He is the seed of woman.

> **And I will put enmity between thee and the woman, and between thy seed and her seed; it shall bruise thy head, and thou shalt bruise his heel.**
>
> Genesis 3:15

God gave this prophecy at the time when He was punishing Adam, Eve, and the serpent for their behavior in the Garden of Eden. Remember, the title deed to the earth was given to Adam by God, but Adam lost it to Satan (the serpent) through sin. So God was speaking to the serpent in Genesis 3:15, telling the serpent that there will be enmity, or hate, antagonism, hostility, between him and the woman. God said that the serpent's seed will bruise the heel of humankind, but Jesus will bruise the head of the serpent.

This Scripture is symbolic of Jesus. The serpent represents Satan, and the seed of woman represents Jesus and humankind. This Scripture tells us that at some point humankind will overcome Satan. We know this time to be when Jesus came to earth as a Man and defeated Satan on the cross.

I think that the beautiful thing about this Scripture is its visualization. For instance, "thou shalt bruise his heel" suggests that Satan will appear to hurt both Jesus and man. Satan has destruction in mind in his attack, but when a serpent attacks a person's heel, it is not untreatable. The heel of a person is a small part of the body, not the leading body part of man.

This reference was fulfilled in Jesus' seemingly ultimate defeat, His death on the cross, when His "heel," or His humanity, was "laid low."[3] Actually, that was God-ordained because our salvation could only be brought about by the death of His beloved Son. But the story doesn't end there—Jesus' encounter with Satan was successful; He won the victory over him.

The reference "he shall bruise thy head" refers to the most significant part of a serpent's body. Did you know that to kill a snake you must smash or sever its head? That is the location of its venom. Although a serpent's bite on a person's heel is dangerous when the poison infects the blood, it is not incurable. But crushing the head of a serpent is destruction for the serpent.[4] Christ bruised the head of the serpent, Satan, when He rose again on the third day, seizing the keys of death and hell.

Jesus truly handicapped Satan's work on this earth, destroying his power and lordship over us and turning us from the power of the enemy to God.[5]

> And having spoiled principalities and powers, he made a shew of them openly, triumphing over them in it.
>
> Colossians 2:15

This prophecy was fulfilled when we saw the seed of a woman—Jesus in human form—bruise the head of Satan.[6]

> And the great dragon was cast out, *that old serpent*, called the Devil, and Satan, which deceiveth the whole world: he was cast out into the earth, and his angels were cast out with him.
>
> And I heard a loud voice saying in heaven, Now is come salvation, and strength, and the kingdom of our God, and the

power of his *Christ:* for the accuser of our brethren is cast
down, which accused them before our God day and night.

And they overcame him by the blood of the Lamb, and by
the word of their testimony; and they loved not their lives
unto the death.

Revelation 12:9-11

If you are ever afraid of what Satan can do in these end
times, get a vision of this passage. It assures us that Jesus will
complete His work in Revelation.

SECOND PROPHECY

The second prophecy forecasts that Jesus will come from the
lineage of Shem. From Shem's descendants come the Jews
bearers of the name "Messiah" to the world. The word *Shem*
even means "name."[7]

And he said, Blessed be the Lord God of Shem; and
Canaan shall be his servant. *God* shall enlarge Japheth,
and *he* shall dwell in the tents of Shem; and Canaan shall
be his servant.

Genesis 9:26,27

What's interesting about this Scripture is that its prophecy
of Jesus lies in the promise of a Messiah. The words, "he shall
dwell in the tents of Shem," refer to a time when Jews and
Gentiles will be in one accord. This time was realized when
Jesus' blood grafted Gentiles spiritually into the covenant
blessings of Abraham.

As one Bible commentary explains, "...Jews and Gentiles
shall be united together in the gospel fold: after many of the

Gentiles shall have been proselyted [converted] to the Jewish religion, both shall be one in Christ, Ephesians 2:14,15. When Japheth joins with Shem, Canaan falls before them both: when strangers become friends, enemies become servants. "[8]

This is one of the end-time mysteries of man that God revealed to John in Revelation:

> And I saw a new heaven and a new earth: for the first heaven and the first earth were passed away; and there was no more sea.
>
> And I John saw the holy city, new Jerusalem, coming down from God out of heaven, prepared as a bride adorned for her husband.
>
> And I heard a great voice out of heaven saying, Behold, the tabernacle of God is with men, and he will dwell with them, and they shall be his people, and God himself shall be with them, and be their God
>
> **Revelation 21:1-3**

Ultimately, Jews and Gentiles will be united together as the final bride of Christ, and they will live together in the new Jerusalem, which has been created by God.

THIRD PROPHECY

The third prophecy referring to Jesus in the book of Genesis revolves around the fact that He is from Abraham's seed.

> And I will make of thee a great nation, and I will bless thee, and make thy name great; and thou shalt be a blessing:
>
> **Genesis 12:2**

And Abraham said, My son, God will provide himself a *lamb* for a burnt offering: so they went both of them together.

And Abraham called the name of that place Jehovahjireh: as it is said *to* this day, In the mount of the Lord it shall be seen.

Genesis 22:8,14

Now to Abraham and his seed were the promises made. He saith not, And to seeds, as of many; but as of one, And to thy seed, which is Christ.

Galatians 3:16

In Genesis 12 God told Abraham that his name would be great. Not only was Abraham's name great as a father of the Jewish nation, but also because his genealogy produced the Savior of the world. Jesus came to save the Jewish people and the Gentiles. However, many of the Jews rejected Jesus as their long-awaited Messiah. In Galatians 3:16 we see that Jesus did come from the lineage of Abraham. In Revelation 7 we witness that 144,000 Jews from every tribe convert to Christ and are part of His church.

Of the tribe of *Juda* were sealed twelve thousand. Of the tribe of *Reuben* were sealed twelve thousand. Of the tribe of *Gad* were sealed twelve thousand.

Of the tribe of *Aser* were sealed twelve thousand. Of the tribe of *Nepthalim* were sealed twelve thousand. Of the tribe of *Manasses* were sealed twelve thousand.

Of the tribe of *Simeon* were sealed twelve thousand. Of the tribe of *Levi* were sealed twelve thousand. Of the tribe of *Issachar* were sealed twelve thousand.

Of the tribe of *Zabulon* were sealed twelve thousand. Of the tribe of *Joseph* were sealed twelve thousand. Of the tribe of *Benjamin* were sealed twelve thousand.

After this I beheld, and, lo, a great multitude, which no man could number, of all nations, and kindreds, and people, and tongues, stood before the throne, and before the Lamb, *clothed with white robes,* and palms in their hands;

And one of the elders answered, saying unto me, What are these which are arrayed in white robes and whence came they?

And I said unto him, Sir, thou knowest. And he said to me, These are they which came out of great tribulation, and *have washed their robes, and made them white in the blood of the Lamb.*

Revelation 7:5-9,13

Because these Jews recognize Jesus as their Messiah, they, along with the Gentiles who believe, will live a triumphant life with Christ for all eternity.

FOURTH PROPHECY

This next verse gives the fourth prophecy of Jesus in Genesis. In it we see Shiloh as being the "rest" for God's people when Jacob prophesied over Judah:

> The sceptre shall not depart from Judah, nor a lawgiver
> from between his feet, until Shiloh come; and unto him
> shall the gathering of the people be.
>
> Genesis 49:10

This Scripture explains that mankind's rest, or Shiloh, will come from the tribe of Judah. In this verse not only does the sceptre symbolize regal, or royal, command,[9] but according to *Unger's Bible Dictionary*, "Shiloh" is "A title of the Messiah ...."[10] We know from our study that God's people will rest—they won't have any more tribulation or distress—at the end when Jesus, "The Prince of Peace,"[11] has come to rule and reign on this earth . That involves Jesus as the Lion of Judah.

> And I heard a voice from heaven saying unto me, Write,
> Blessed are the dead which die in the Lord from hence-
> forth: Yea, saith the Spirit, that they may *rest from their
> labours;* and their works do follow them.
>
> Revelation 14: 13

Jesus fulfills this prophecy of man's rest in His portrayal as the Lion of Judah in Revelation 5:5:

> And one of the elders saith unto me, Weep nor: behold, the
> *Lion of the tribe of Juda, the Root of David,* hath prevailed
> to open the book, and to loose the seven seals thereof.

Bible scholar Albert Barnes talks of the significance of the Messiah being called the Lion of the tribe of Judah, saying," ...This use of the term would connect him in the apprehension of John with the prophecy, and would suggest to him the idea of his being a ruler, or having dominion ...."[12]

Drawing on these Scriptures and scriptural principles establishes the fact that the Lion of Judah appears on earth "conquering and to conquer."[13] In "ruling, or having dominion " on earth (as He does in heaven), Jesus, who is a Man of rest, will bring rest and peace to the people of God.

OUR ROLE IN HIS-STORY

God's major goal will not be finished until the whole world is in its original state and back to its original Owner. First Corinthians 15:25 tells us that Christ must reign until all enemies are under His feet.

Once that is accomplished, the saints will reign with Him, judging the inhabitants of the world.

> **Do you not know that the saints [the believers] will [one day] judge and govern the world? And if the world [itself] is to be judged and ruled by you, are you unworthy and incompetent to try [such petty matters] of the smallest courts of justice?**
>
> **1 Corinthians 6:2 AMP**

Some Bible scholars feel that this verse does not necessarily mean that we will literally judge the world and condemn the wicked. It is more likely that the world's civil government will be administered by Christians.[14] Either way, until that time the preaching of the Word and the program of redemption is committed to the body of Christ.

We are a part of God's grand plan of redemption. Our job is to watch for the great move of God that is coming, but not passively. We need to put into action what we know and boldly spread the Gospel message, because what Satan has in mind for this world is going to be devastating for those who are left behind in the first Rapture. Remember, he doesn't want to give up the earth, so he devises a vile game plan to thwart God's master blueprint for humanity.

God doesn't want us to be ignorant of His end-time plan, and He doesn't want us to be ignorant of Satan's devices. Next, we're going to meet the Antichrist, one of Satan's most powerful "tools," who is instrumental in his plan for world control. But God is more than big enough, strong enough, and powerful enough to break up his evil scheme. God's vision for our future guarantees victory!

SECTION 3

THE ANTICHRIST

CHAPTER 5

WHO IS THE ANTICHRIST?

For centuries people have wondered about the identity of the Antichrist. Some have even guessed he was an infamous world ruler. Names such as Napoleon, Hitler, and Mussolini have been tossed into the hat for possible Antichrist candidates. But I am not going to try to name him. I prefer to look at the Scriptures surrounding his identity and take our cue from their wisdom.

We first encounter the Antichrist in the book of Genesis and continue reading about him through Revelation. We must be aware of these Scriptures in order to know about his rise to power because he is a key personality who has a significant role in the end times.

From the first three chapters of Revelation, we know that we are currently living in the last segment of the Church Age. I believe that because we are living in the end of the age when Jesus returns, the Antichrist could be alive today.

Let me emphasize that there is no reason to fear the Antichrist any more than there is a reason to fear the devil.

According to the Word, he is a defeated foe. The only fear we are supposed to have is the fear, or reverence, of God. When you know who His Son Jesus is and what He's done for you, it just comes naturally. And Proverbs 9:10 tells us that the fear of God is the beginning of wisdom. That wisdom is essential for living in the last days and for a fulfilling Christian life.

It is wisdom to educate ourselves on the details the Scriptures provide about the Antichrist so that we are not ignorant of Satan's devices. Understanding the Antichrist's role in the dramatic events of the last days is an important part of our mandate to watch and pray.

One passage that describes the Antichrist is 1 John 2:18,22.

Little children, it is the last time: and as ye have heard that antichrist shall come, even now are there many antichrists; whereby we know that it is the last time.

Who is a liar but he that denieth that Jesus is the Christ? He is antichrist, that denieth the Father and the Son.

Notice verse 18 warns us not only of the Antichrist, but also of many antichrists to come. This is one of the main ways Christians will recognize the end is near.

RULING SYSTEMS

While there is only one Antichrist who will fulfill John's vision in Revelation, there are many antichrists of lesser significance (but still treacherous and misleading) in today's society who are examples of the spirit of antichrist working in the world.

For instance, there are ruling systems against Christ, such as Communism. This theory and system of social and political organization was a major force in world politics during much of the twentieth century and still has some single-parry communist countries in existence today.

Communistic governments eliminate the freedom of religion and Christianity from its people. Any government system that is against Christ can be considered antichrist.

PEOPLE/MOVEMENTS

Throughout history, various individuals and movements have reflected the spirit of antichrist. Secular humanism and New Age movements promote life without a dependence on God. These movements teach that humankind is supreme in ourselves, without need of any outside creator or divine being. This antichrist spirit works even today to infiltrate the minds of individuals.

Other infamous people in history exemplified the spirit of antichrist. Hitler provides us with a strong example of this. His hatred for God's people, the Jews, marked one of the cruelest atrocities in history.

While the spirit of the antichrist is seen in various realms of influence today, there is still only one Antichrist. He is the one we are going to focus on in the remainder of this chapter.

The Bible refers to the Antichrist by many names. We just saw in 1 John 2:18,22 that he is identified by the first name— Antichrist.

I want to talk about some of the other names because it will help develop his character for you and give you a profile of him (what he will be like, what he'll do, his personality), although I won't try to say specifically who he is.

Some of these names are symbolic references to him. Remember, God uses symbols in His Word to paint a visual picture of divine concepts. This kind of biblical symbolism helps us to comprehend and hold on to the principles of God.

FIRST NAME—"ANTICHRIST"

What does the term *Antichrist* mean? Dividing the word, we see two parts: anti and Christ. Simply put, *anti* means "opposed to: AGAINST."[1] *Christ* means "Messiah."[2] Basically, the name *Antichrist* means "against Christ." So, according to the meaning of his name, he is against Jesus Christ. And he will live up to his name.

When the Antichrist arrives on the public scene, he will attempt to emulate Christ by eventually seeking to position himself in Jesus' place.

SECOND NAME—"LITTLE HORN"

I considered the horns, and, behold, there came up among them another *little* horn, before whom there were three of the first horns plucked up by the roots: and, behold, in this horn were eyes like the eyes of man, and a mouth speaking great things.

And out of one of them came forth a *little horn*, which waxed exceeding great, toward the south, and toward the east, and toward the pleasant land.

Daniel 7:8; 8:9

The second name the Bible gives the Antichrist is "little horn." We see this name in the book of Daniel during two of Daniel's visions, both of which reveal end-time events. I believe Daniel called the Antichrist "little horn"[3] because the Antichrist will exalt himself.

Daniel gives a wonderful description of what is going to happen with nations and world empires in the end time. His visions even provide a good idea of the general location from where the Antichrist could come.

In Daniel's vision, he predicted the rise of ten kingdoms. Out of those kingdoms, one kingdom (belonging to the Antichrist) will rise and conquer three of the others because the Antichrist will have great power to make war. Then the other seven kingdoms will say to him, "Don't fight with us! We will just come along with you!" What does he do really well to make people follow him? He knows how to make war.

Before we look at the third name of the Antichrist, let's look at a dream that the Babylonian ruler King Nebuchadnezzar had. Understanding this king's dream will help us to understand the meaning of Daniel's vision and things to come in the last days.

NEBUCHADNEZZAR'S DREAM

During the Jewish captivity in Babylon (which is present-day Iraq), the ruling King Nebuchadnezzar received a dream that troubled his spirit. (Dan. 2:1.) Unfortunately, he could not remember his dream when he awoke. Frustrated and angry, he demanded that the wise men of Babylon recall and explain his dream or suffer a vicious death.

When Daniel learned of this plan, he went in to see the king and asked him to give him a little time, and he would tell the king his dream and what it meant. Then Daniel went home and petitioned God to reveal the dream to him. In a vision, God revealed Nebuchadnezzar's dream and the interpretation to Daniel, thus sparing the lives of all the wise men. Daniel praised God's sovereignty and wisdom, exclaiming:

> ... Blessed be the name of God for ever and ever: for wisdom and might are his:

> And he changeth the times and the seasons: he removeth kings, and setteth up kings: he giveth wisdom unto the wise, and knowledge to them that know understanding:

> He revealeth the deep and secret things: he knoweth what is in the darkness, and the light dwelleth with him.

> I thank thee, and praise thee, O thou God of my fathers, who hast given me wisdom and might, and hast made known unto me now what we desired of thee: for thou hast now made known unto us the king's matter.
> Daniel 2:20-24

After asking mercy for the wise men, Daniel was brought to the king, and he told the king the dream and interpreted it.

In his dream, Nebuchadnezzar saw a four-part creature. (vv. 31-45.) The head was gold, the arms were silver, the belly was brass, the legs were iron, and the feet were a mix of iron and clay. Daniel's interpretation of this dream illustrated the major world empires predicted for the future. Daniel explained that the golden head represented Babylon. Babylon was to be the first world empire.[4]

Notice in this example, gold is the most precious metal. The first empire in Nebuchadnezzar's dream is gold and each empire decreases in metallic worth as we look down the creature's body. The silver arms represent the Medes and Persians—a two-part empire. The stomach of brass represents Greece. The two legs of iron are the Roman Empire.

Finally, you could say that the creature's two legs extend down into the end times, and we see ten toes. The ten toes are made of clay and iron.

I believe that these ten toes represent the ten kingdoms that spring forth from the Roman Empire.[5] These kingdoms are the revived Roman Empire during the end times. You may wonder where the Roman Empire is located. It is in Europe, parts of the Middle East, and parts of Africa.

The revived Roman Empire will encompass the area around the Mediterranean Sea. According to Bible prophecy, the ten kingdoms that are going to rise out of the Roman Empire will be from this area.

THE CRUSHING STONE

Suddenly, there is a turning point in the king's dream. A stone smashes the feet of the creature and brings down the entire structure.

> Thou sawest till that a stone was cut out without hands, which smote the image upon his feet that were of iron and clay, and brake them to pieces.
>
> Then was the iron, the clay, the brass, the silver, and the gold, broken to pieces together, and became like the chaff of the summer threshing floors; and the wind carried them away, that no place was found for them: and the

stone that smote the image became a great mountain, and
filled the whole earth.

Daniel 2:34,35

This stone represents Jesus Christ and His kingdom. As
one Bible commentary describes it, "...In its relation to Israel
it is a 'stone of stumbling' (Isa. 8:14...) on which both houses
of Israel are 'broken,' not destroyed, as Antichrist and his fac-
tion shall be (Matt. 21:42,44...). In its relation to the Church,
the same stone which destroys the image is the foundation of
the Church (Eph. 2:20). In its relation to the Gentile world-
power [the Antichrist], the stone is its destroyer...."[6]

Notice that the stone did not just crush the toes; the whole
statue fell. In history, we know that each empire fell. Babylon
fell to the Medes and the Persians. The Medes and the Persians fell to Greece. The Greek Empire fell to the Romans.

However, when we see the ten toes, the stone crushes the
entire statue. Many agree on what this symbolizes—that the
ten nations that used to be a part of the old Roman Empire
(including historical Babylon, Medes and Persia, Greece,
and Rome) are going to rise again in Europe. This area of the
world is going to become very strong in end-time politics,
geography, and war.

It is from one of those ten nations that the "little horn,"
or leader, will arise. This leader will be very skillful at making
war, and he will fight. His skills of warfare will attract people
to follow him. This will begin his reign of deception.

The number one tool the Antichrist will use is deception.

We do not see this little horn mentioned in the above references of King Nebuchadnezzar's dream. You may be wondering

where that little horn's tie to the ten kingdoms comes from. It is taken from two other visions that Daniel experienced.

In these visions, the Lord expounded on King Nebuchadnezzar's dream of the four empires.[7] I'm not going to go into much detail here except to say that the little horn will surface from these empires. As we have seen, he will be strong and powerful, and he will lead by deception. He will end up conquering three of the little kingdoms and then will begin to grow in popularity and power.

Eventually he will become greater than the country he came from and will desire imperial power. This will cause him to conquer the ten kingdoms from that part of the Mediterranean world. (Remember, this little horn represents the Antichrist and corresponds to the message portrayed in King Nebuchadnezzar's dream.)

After the little horn, or Antichrist, arises from the ten kingdoms, a crushing stone will take him down. We will discuss this more later on, but as we just saw, this stone represents the kingdom of Jesus Christ.

THIRD NAME—"VILE PERSON"

The third name the Bible gives the Antichrist is "vile person." Daniel spoke about this "vile person" during one of his visions:

> **And in his estate shall stand up a vile person, to whom they shall not give the honour of the kingdom: but he shall come in peaceably, and obtain the kingdom by flatteries.**
> **Daniel 11:21**

This verse was describing something that happened in the life of Antiochus IV Epiphanes, who represents the Antichrist.

He persecuted the Jews and desecrated the temple, foreshadowing the offenses that the Antichrist will commit against the Jewish people.[8]

In this Scripture Daniel warned that the Antichrist, or vile person, will utilize flattery to overcome nations. The Hebrew word in this passage for *vile person* makes an interesting point. The word is *bazah* which is a title given to a person who "despises the Lord [and] is devious in his ways. "[9] This undoubtedly portrays the Antichrist as someone who will outwardly despise anything having to do with God and His people. It will be evident in his actions towards the people of God during the Tribulation.

Also significant is the fact that although the Antichrist is described by the Bible as being a vile person, he is able to use peaceable methods to build his empire. Notice in verse 21 the Bible says that he uses flatteries. This again proves his method of operation is deceit.

The unsuspecting kingdoms will be given over to the Antichrist. They will not realize they are giving control to a vile person. The Antichrist will use deception to manipulate and gain control. It is only in the latter part of the Tribulation that his true colors will be revealed.

FOURTH NAME—"ASSYRIAN"

And the Lord shall cause his glorious voice to be heard, and shall shew the lighting down of his arm, with the

indignation of his anger, and with the flame of a devouring fire, with scattering, and tempest, and hailstones.

For through the voice of the Lord shall the Assyrian be beaten down, which smote with a rod.

Isaiah 30:30,31

O Assyrian, the rod of mine anger, and the staff in their hand is mine indignation.

I will send him against an hypocritical nation, and against the people of my wrath will I give him a charge, to take the spoil, and to take the prey, and to tread them down like the mire of the streets.

Howbeit he meaneth not so, neither doth his heart think so; but it is in his heart to destroy and cut off nations not a few.

Isaiah 10:5-7

The term "Assyrian" in these passages is generally considered to be a symbolic representation of the Antichrist. In calling him the "Assyrian," Isaiah gives some indication of where he will emerge, but opinions vary on this. He could be a Jew born somewhere within the borders of the old Assyrian empire, although it's doubtful. It is more likely that he will come from one of the European countries that was once part of the Old Roman Empire. No one knows for sure.

FIFTH NAME—"GOG AND MAGOG"

And the word of the Lord came unto me, saying,

Son of man, set thy face against Gog, the land of Magog, the chief prince of Meshech and Tubal, and prophesy against him,

And say, Thus saith the Lord God; Behold, I am against thee, O Gog, the chief prince of Meshech and Tubal:

And I will turn thee back, and put hooks into thy jaws, and I will bring thee forth, and all thine army, horses and horse men, all of them clothed with all sorts of armour, even a great company with bucklers and shields, all of them handling swords.

Ezekiel 3 8: 1-4

Here we see Ezekiel describing him as the chief prince of the countries of Meshech and Tubal. Originally, Meshech and Tubal weren't countries; they were grandsons of Noah who settled near the Black and Caspian seas, which are currently bounded by Syria, Turkey, Romania, the Ukraine, Iran, Iraq, and others.

Many people think that "Gog" and "Magog" are the names of Russia, but I don't think that at all. Some Bible scholars believe that they refer to the Antichrist in the sense that Gog and Magog represent all those who oppose Jesus, that they symbolize the anti-Christian forces on the earth.[10]

I agree that Gog and Magog have to do with Satan and his power through Antichrist in the sense that "Gog" has to do with Satan and "Magog" has to do with the Antichrist who comes out of Satan warring and fighting.

SIXTH NAME—"MAN OF SIN"

Now we beseech you, brethren, by the coming of our Lord Jesus Christ, and by our gathering together unto him,

That ye be not soon shaken in mind, or be troubled, neither by spirit, nor by word, nor by letter as from us, as that the day of Christ is at hand.

Let no man deceive you by any means: for that day shall not come, except there come a falling away first, and that *man of sin* be revealed, the son of perdition;

Who opposeth and exalteth himself above all that is called God, or that is worshipped; so that he as God sitteth in the temple of God, shewing himself that he is God.

Remember ye not, that, when I was yet with you, I told you these things?

2 Thessalonians 2:1-5

The apostle Paul in his letter to the Thessalonians mentioned the name, "man of sin," to them. Paul was directly answering misunderstandings concerning the timing of the events of the end times. He told the Thessalonians not to listen to rumors and reports that the day of the Lord had already begun because a number of events must occur before Christ returns. For one thing, there will be a great rebellion against God led by the man of sin (or lawlessness), the Antichrist.[11] And God will remove all the restraints on evil before He brings judgment on the rebels.[12]

The Antichrist is referred to as the "man of sin" because everything he will work to accomplish on earth will be opposite of God. He will conduct affairs lawlessly and without restraint. The Antichrist is a true picture of sin incarnate.

SEVENTH NAME—"BEAST"

In Revelation 13 the Bible describes the Antichrist as "a beast."

> And I stood upon the sand of the sea, and saw a beast rise up out of the sea, having seven heads and ten horns, and upon his horns ten crowns, and upon his heads the name of blasphemy.
>
> Revelation 13:1

The beast in Chapter 13 actually refers to two key end-time personalities represented by a first and second beast. The first is the Antichrist, the future political ruler who will oppose God and all of His followers; the second is the false prophet, the future religious ruler who will force the world to worship the Antichrist (the first beast). This next passage gives a very clear picture of what the Antichrist as both will seek to accomplish.[13]

> And they worshipped the dragon which gave power unto the beast: and they worshipped the beast, saying, Who is like unto the beast? who is able to make war with him?
>
> And there was given unto him a mouth speaking great things and blasphemies; and power was given unto him to continue forty and two months.
>
> And he opened his mouth in blasphemy against God, to blaspheme his name, and his tabernacle, and them that dwell in heaven.

And it was given unto him to make war with the saints, and to overcome them: and power was given him over all kindreds, and tongues, and nations.

And all that dwell upon the earth shall worship him, whose names are not written in the book of life of the Lamb slain from the foundation of the world.

Revelation 13:4-8

In verses 11-15 we read about the beast again. This second reference (of the Antichrist as the beast) refers to the false prophet, the religious ruler who will force the world to worship the Antichrist as the first beast mentioned in this passage.

And I beheld another beast coming up out of the earth; and he had two horns like a lamb, and he spake as a dragon.

And he exerciseth all the power of the first beast before him, and causeth the earth and them which dwell therein to worship the first beast, whose deadly wound was healed.

And he docth great wonders, so that he maketh fire come down from heaven on the earth in the sight of men,

And deceiveth them that dwell on the earth by the means of those miracles which he had power to do in the sight of the beast; saying to them that dwell on the earth, that they should make an image to the beast, which had the wound by a sword, and did live.

And he had power to give life unto the image of the beast, that the image of the beast should both speak, and cause that as many as would not worship the image of the beast should be killed.

The Antichrist is also called "beast" in Revelation 17:3. John wrote, "So he carried me away in the spirit into the wilderness: and I saw a woman sit upon a scarlet coloured beast, full of names of blasphemy, having seven heads and ten horns."

Notice John was in the Spirit when he saw the beast. Remember, we studied earlier about the significance of John receiving the vision of Revelation from the Holy Spirit. How did John recognize the beast? He was able to identify the beast from the guidance of the Holy Spirit.

The Antichrist is always opposite of Jesus. We know that Jesus is the Lamb; therefore, is it any surprise that the Antichrist is the beast?

EIGHTH NAME—"OF TYRE"

The Antichrist will be a great builder of cities. He will even rebuild Tyre and Babylon. Tyre was located in what is now southern Lebanon on the Mediterranean Sea; Babylon was located in present day Iraq.

It is interesting to me that in the Old Testament the kings of Tyre and Babylon both claimed worship as divine beings. (Dan. 3:1-12.)[14] They made their people bow down to them because they wanted to be treated as gods. Isn't that a long-held ambition of Satan right from the beginning? Hasn't he always been attempting to be like God?

Remember, Satan's ambition will be temporarily satisfied when he, in the form of the Antichrist, will be worshiped by all who are left on the earth after the Rapture.

NINTH NAME—"SON OF PERDITION"

The Antichrist is a man empowered by Satan. Among his many names in the Bible is the "son of perdition."

> Let no man deceive you by any means: for that day shall not come, except there come a falling away first, and that man of sin be revealed, the *son of perdition;*
>
> Who opposeth and exalteth himself above all that is called God, or that is worshipped; so that he as God sitteth in the temple of God, shewing himself that he is God.
>
> 2 Thessalonians 2:3,4

> And every spirit that confesseth not that Jesus Christ is come in the flesh is not of God: and this is that spirit of antichrist, whereof ye have heard that it should come; and even now already is it in the world.
>
> 1 John 4:3

Another person in the Bible who is referred to as the son of perdition is Judas Iscariot.[15] Some believe that it is possible the Antichrist may be Judas Iscariot returning to earth in an action that counterfeits Jesus' return to earth. This idea is not often talked about, but because it is possible, let's look at some of the reasoning behind it.

A double prophecy in Psalm 55 shows both Judas's betrayal of Jesus[16] and the Antichrist's betrayal of Israel, revealing them to be the same man. And Luke 22:3 says, "Then entered Satan into Judas surnamed Iscariot...." Jesus called Judas a devil, which suggests that Judas was more than a man.

Jesus answered them, Have not I chosen you twelve, and one of you is a devil?

John 6:70

The original Greek translation for the word Jesus used to describe Judas in this verse is "diabolos," which means "false accuser," "slanderer." It is one of the names of Satan.[17]

Matthew Henry's Bible commentary refers to Judas as the devil, saying, "Hypocrites and betrayers of Christ are no better than devils. Judas not only had a devil, but he was a devil. One of you is a false accuser; so diabolos sometimes signifies (2 Tim. 3:3); and it is probable that Judas, when he sold his Master to the chief priests, represented him to them as a bad man, to justify himself in what he did. But I rather take it as we read it: He is a devil, a devil incarnate, a fallen apostle, as the devil a fallen angel. He is Satan, an adversary, an enemy to Christ. He is Abaddon, and Apollyon, a son of perdition. He was of his father the devil, did his lusts, was in his interests, as Cain, (1 John 3:12). Those whose bodies were possessed by the devil are never called devils (demoniacs, but not devils); but Judas, into whose heart Satan entered, and filled it, is called a devil."[18]

Was Judas the devil incarnate, just as the Lord Jesus was God incarnate? In John 17:12 Jesus Himself calls Judas the "son of perdition."

While I was with them in the world, I kept them in thy name: those that thou gavest me I have kept, and none of them is lost, but the *son of perdition;* that the scripture might be fulfilled.

John 17:12

This is the same name Paul called the Antichrist in 2 Thessalonians 2:3, as we saw earlier.

Another interesting concept based upon Scripture is that the Antichrist will ascend from the same place Judas Iscariot went upon death.[19]

> **And when they shall have finished their testimony, the beast that ascendeth out of the bottomless pit shall make war against them, and shall overcome them, and kill them.**
>
> Revelation 11:7

The Antichrist will come from hell and will be super-human. In Revelation 11:7 he is seen coming out of the bottomless pit, which is the abode of lost spirits and wicked dead, the place of their incarceration and torment.[20] The Antichrist will come from the bottomless pit where Judas Iscariot was sent when he died.

Taking all this into consideration, I think it is possible that the Antichrist's history as Judas Iscariot is revealed in Revelation 17:8.

> **The beast that thou sawest was, and is not; and shall ascend out of the bottomless pit, and go into perdition: and they that dwell on the earth shall wonder, whose names were not written in the book of life from the foundation of the world, when they behold the beast that was, and is not, and yet is.**

From the last line of this Scripture we can see that the Antichrist was once on earth (possibly in the form of Judas) and then, in John's day, he was not on earth possibly because he was dead (when Judas hanged himself). He will ascend out of the bottomless pit at the time of his rebirth (as the Antichrist) and end up in perdition when Jesus casts him in the Lake of Fire at Armageddon.

TENTH NAME—THE CHALDEAN

I believe that Habakkuk gives quite a description of the Antichrist in this passage (symbolically speaking).

"Look among the nations! Observe! Be astonished! Wonder! Because [I] am doing something in your days—you would not believe if you were told.

"For behold, I am raising up the Chaldeans, that fierce and impetuous people who march throughout the earth to seize dwelling places which are not theirs.

"They are dreaded and feared. Their justice and authority originate with themselves.

"Their horses are swifter than leopards and keener than wolves in the evening. Their horsemen come galloping, their horsemen come from afar; they fly like an eagle swooping [down] to devour.

"All of them come for violence. Their horde of faces [moves] forward. They collect captives like sand.

"They mock at kings, and rulers are a laughing matter to them. They laugh at every fortress, and heap up rubble to capture it.

"Then they will sweep through [like] the wind and pass on. But they will be held guilty, they whose strength is their god."

Art Thou not from everlasting, O Lord, my God, my Holy One? We will not die. Thou, O Lord, hast appointed them to judge; and Thou, O Rock, hast established them to correct.

[Thine] eyes are too pure to approve evil, and Thou canst not look on wickedness [with favor.] Why dost Thou look with favor On those who deal treacherously? Why art Thou silent when the wicked swallow up those more righteous than they?

[Why] hast Thou made men like the fish of the sea, like creeping things without a ruler over them?

[The Chaldeans] bring all of them up with a hook, drag them away with their net, and gather them together in their fishing net. Therefore, they rejoice and are glad.

Therefore, they offer a sacrifice to their net. And burn incense to their fishing net; because through these things their catch is large, and their food is plentiful.

Will they therefore empty their net and continually slay nations without sparing?

Habakkuk 1:5-17 NAS

Chaldean and *Babylonian* refer to the same people. The Chaldeans are better known as the Babylonians, and we've already seen that "Babylonian" is another name for the Antichrist .

Habakkuk wrote this passage because he was very troubled about the evil and injustice overtaking his land at the hands of the Chaldeans. The violent Chaldean "nation," or end-time Antichrist figure, may have plans to bring calamity on our present world, but God has an intended end for every

trial and an intended "after."[21] There will be new life and blessings after Armageddon and the Tribulation because God can
even use the wicked to bring His purposes forth.

Are you beginning to get the picture of the type of person
the Antichrist will be? As we will see next, the Antichrist is a
counterfeit of Jesus in every way.

CHAPTER 6

PORTRAIT OF EVIL

The Antichrist is completely opposite of everything Jesus represents. Satan always tries to counterfeit everything that God does, only whatever he does is never of God; it's the devil's realm. According to the Bible, he even has a counterfeit trinity. Of course, God has the holy trinity—God the Father, God the Son (Jesus), and God the Holy Spirit. Well, the devil has his satanic trinity mentioned in Revelation 16:13, which is comprised of:

- The Dragon—Satan
- The Antichrist—the beast
- The False Prophet

Satan uses counterfeiting as a method to draw people off course. When we do not educate ourselves on exactly what the Word says, it is easy to miss the subtle differences. Deception is a very subtle thing, and we're going to see it more and more in our day. But if we cling to the Word, we won't be deceived.

When all the end-time events take place, it's going to be a tremendous testimony to the world that the Word of God is true. So Satan has to come up with some big-time miraculous, counterfeit measures to try to overcome that.

Satan has always used the counterfeiting method to confuse the world of God's plan. We see this happen throughout the Bible. As watchers, we must stay focused (on God) to avoid confusion. Here's an example of what having the right focus can do.

I heard of a woman who swam the English Channel and wanted to set a record, but when she was a half a mile from the shore, she became exhausted. Her coach, her mom, and some friends were following her in a boat, so she called for them to bring the boat over to her so she could climb in. But they said to her, "Oh, don't stop now! You only have half a mile from the shore!"

She couldn't see the land because it was really foggy; she just saw the fog, and that's what she focused on. She said to them, "I think you're wrong. I think it's farther than half a mile, and I see all that fog. I just can't go on."

When she got into the boat and discovered that it really was only half a mile to shore, she said to them, "If I could have seen the land, I would not have stopped. But when I saw that fog I thought, *Oh it's much farther*, and I just didn't finish it." Instead of holding on until the end, standing to the end, swimming to the end, she lost it by just such a little margin because she had the wrong focus.

The next year she went into the contest and swam the English Channel again. It was foggy again, but she had a new strategy. This time she didn't focus on the fog; she focused on finishing, and not only did she finish, but she beat all the records by two hours. She was the fastest one to swim the English Channel—she finished the course because she stayed focused.

God has a strategy for us to stay focused—stay saturated in the Word. That way, we will be able to recognize the enemy's counterfeits and finish our course victoriously—the way God has promised us we can finish.

There's a special Scripture passage that illustrates this so well. Matthew 13:26-30 tells how Jesus went forth to sow the good seed, and Satan's counterfeit was to immediately sow tares. With God's help, and by staying in His Word, we will not be deceived by the enemy.

> **For it is God which worketh in you both to will and to do of his good pleasure.**
>
> **Philippians 2:13**

> **Wherein in time past ye walked according to the course of this world, according to the prince of the power of the air, the spirit that now worketh in the children of disobedience.**
>
> **Ephesians 2:2**

Notice in Ephesians 2:2 who will be deceived. Those who follow the Antichrist and fall for his counterfeits are going to be the disobedient. When you refuse the truth (of God's Word), what will you believe but a lie? In fact, one of Satan's counterfeits is what the Bible calls "another gospel."

COUNTERFEIT MESSAGE

And Jesus went about all Galilee, teaching in their syn-
agogues, and *preaching the gospel* of the kingdom, and
healing all manner of sickness and all manner of disease
among the people.

Matthew 4:23

And saying, The time is fulfilled, and the kingdom of God
is at hand: repent ye, and believe the *gospel.*

Mark 1:15

Jesus came to bring *the* Gospel, the Good News. However,
Satan has another gospel, or counterfeit message, he will seek
to spread.

But I fear, lest by any means, as the serpent beguiled Eve
through his subtilty, so your minds should be corrupted
from the simplicity that is in Christ.

For if he that cometh preacheth another Jesus, whom we
have not preached, or if ye receive another spirit, which
ye have not received, or *another gospel,* which ye have not
accepted, ye might well bear with him.

2 Corinthians 11:3,4

So the Antichrist will come with another gospel and
as another Jesus. Empowered by Satan, the Antichrist will
attempt to counterfeit the One true Savior.

We see this in the Antichrist's counterfeit of his followers. We know from the Word that Jesus led twelve disciples
during His ministry on earth.

And when it was day, he called unto him his disciples: and *of them he chose twelve, whom also he named apostles.*

Luke 6:13

But did you know that Satan has his "apostles," too?

And I will keep on doing what I am doing in order to cut the ground from under those who want an opportunity to be considered equal with us in the things they boast about.

For such men are *false apostles*, deceitful workmen, masquerading as apostles of Christ.

And no wonder, for Satan himself masquerades as an angel of light.

It is not surprising, then, if his servants masquerade as servants of righteousness....

2 Corinthians 11:12-15 NIV

...and thou hast tried them which say they are *apostles*, and are not, and hast found them liars:

Revelation 2:2

The Bible states that God will seal His servants on the forehead.

And it was commanded them that they should not hurt the grass of the earth, neither any green thing, neither any tree; but only those men which have not the *seal of God in their foreheads.*

Revelation 9:4

Based on what we already know about the Antichrist, it should come as no surprise that he will have a counterfeit of this, requiring his followers to also take a seal, or mark, on their foreheads.

> And the third angel followed them, saying with a loud voice, If any man worship the beast and his image, and receive his *mark in his forehead,* or in his hand.
>
> Revelation 14:9

Why does Satan do all of this counterfeiting? He is jealous of God's kingdom and people. If he can confuse or persuade people to follow him, then he thinks he has won.

Many times the church only knows "enough to be dangerous" about the facts of the Bible. This makes it very easy for Satan to confuse and lead some away. As we've seen, that is why we must study and understand God's warnings and truths. The Bible is God's Word to mankind. It tells us who we are and how we should live, especially in this last hour. It comforts, guides, and instructs us daily. We can find wisdom, encouragement, and the answers we've been looking for in the Bible.

Remember, the Antichrist's personality is fundamentally opposed to Christ's. Satan himself is transformed into an angel of light. However, through Scripture we know that Jesus is the true Light of the world.[1]

BIG MOUTH, PIERCING EYES

> And of the ten horns that were in his head, and of the other which came up, and before whom three fell; even of that horn that had eyes, and a mouth that spake very great things, whose look was more stout than his fellows.
>
> Daniel 7:20

This verse reveals to us that the Antichrist will exalt himself and speak tremendous things, but he won't speak the truth, and he will have a look that is "stout" or strong, firm, and forceful. This Old Testament Scripture can be cross-compared with a New Testament Scripture in Revelation.

> And there was given unto him a mouth speaking great things and blasphemies; and power was given unto him to continue forty and two months.
>
> Revelation 13:5

This man will be an oratorical genius. Evidenced by his later successes in the political, economical, and warfare realms, the Antichrist will use his great speaking ability and charm to persuade nations to follow him.

FIERCE AND INTELLIGENT

The Antichrist will possess great intelligence. In the book of Daniel, we read that he will have an intense expression that stands out. Daniel mentioned this from one of his many visions.

> ...a king of fierce countenance, and understanding dark sentences, shall stand up.
>
> Daniel 8:23

The Hebrew word for *fierce* in this Scripture is "az," which has several meanings—strong, fierce, mighty, power, greedy, and roughly.[2] In this particular Scripture, it is being applied to a human—the Antichrist. When this word is applied to people, it seems invariably to denote enemies.[3] Obviously, this "fierce countenance" characteristic of the Antichrist is an attribute of the enemies of God.

This verse also says that the Antichrist will understand dark sentences (referring to his skill in trickery, intrigue, and stratagem)[4] and hard questions. In other words, he will be crafty, shrewd, seeking to make his way and to accomplish his purpose, not only by the terror that he will inspire, but by deceit and cunning.[5]

Daniel's prophecies reveal the Antichrist's traits and God's plan for Israel's future.[6] This great antagonist who will fill the world with wickedness will be so far above anyone else on earth that, as the next passage reveals, it will take divine intervention from God to stop him.

> "Toward the end of their kingdoms, when they have become morally rotten, an angry king shall rise to power with great shrewdness and intelligence.
>
> His power shall be mighty, but it will be satanic strength and not his own. Prospering wherever he turns, he will destroy all who oppose him, though their armies be mighty, and he will devastate God's people.
>
> "He will be a master of deception, defeating many by catching them off guard as they bask in false security. Without warning he will destroy them. So great will he fancy himself to be that he will even take on the Prince of Princes in battle; but in so doing he will seal his own doom, for he shall be broken by the hand of God, though no human means could overpower him.
>
> Daniel 8:23-25 TLB

This description of the Antichrist suggests that he will be wiser than Daniel and Ezekiel because he will know the answers to great secrets and possess unusual intelligence. Be assured that when the Antichrist finally arises, he will be greatly admired for his extraordinary intellect.

No wonder so many will be deceived if they don't know the Word. Let's look at some more specific areas illustrated in the Bible in which the Antichrist will excel.

SEVEN AREAS OF INTELLIGENCE

The world will accept the Antichrist because he will be a genius in seven areas. I'm going to unveil them through Scriptures.

Intellect

> Behold, thou art wiser than Daniel; there is no secret that they can hide from thee:
>
> Ezekiel 28:3

> And in the latter time of their kingdom, when the transgressors are come to the full, a king of fierce countenance, and understanding dark sentences, shall stand up.
>
> Daniel 8:23

Oration

> And of the ten horns that were in his head, and of the other which came up, and before whom three fell; even of that horn that had eyes, and a mouth that spake very great things, whose look was more stout than his fellows.
>
> Daniel 7:20

And the beast which I saw was like unto a leopard, and his feet were as the feet of a bear, and his mouth as the mouth of a lion: and the dragon gave him his power, and his seat, and great authority.

Revelation 13:2

Politics

And in his estate shall stand up a vile person, to whom they shall not give the honour of the kingdom: but he shall come in peaceably, and obtain the kingdom by flatteries.

Daniel 11:21

For God hath put in their hearts to fulfil his will, and to agree, and give their kingdom unto the beast, until the words of God shall be fulfilled.

Revelation 17:17

Commerce

With thy wisdom and with thine understanding thou hast gotten thee riches, and hast gotten gold and silver into thy treasures:

By thy great wisdom and by thy traffick hast thou increased thy riches, and thine heart is lifted up because of thy riches.

Ezekiel 28:4,5

And through his policy also he shall cause craft to prosper in his hand; and he shall magnify himself in his heart, and by peace shall destroy many: he shall also stand up against the Prince of princes; but he shall be broken without hand.

Daniel 8:25

But in his estate shall he honour the God of forces: and a god whom his fathers knew nor shall he honour with gold, and silver, and with precious stones, and pleasant things.

But he shall have power over the treasures of gold and of silver, and over all the precious things of Egypt: and the Libyans and the Ethiopians shall be at his steps.

Daniel 11:38,43

Military and Government

They that see thee shall narrowly look upon thee, and consider thee, saying, Is this the man that made the earth to tremble, that did shake kingdoms;

That made the world as a wilderness, and destroyed the cities thereof; that opened not the house of his prisoners?

Isaiah 14:16,17

And his power shall be mighty, bur not by his own power: and he shall destroy wonderfully, and shall prosper, and practise, and shall destroy the mighty and the holy people.

Daniel 8:24

Religion

Who opposeth and exalteth himself above all that is called God, or that is worshipped; so that he as God sitteth in the temple of God, shewing himself that he is God.

2 Thessalonians 2:4

When you read of all these awful attributes and exploits, you may think, *This is just terrible*. But when they begin to happen, they will just be signs that things are about to wrap up.

THE ANTICHRIST'S ORIGIN

Many people have asked me, "Where is the Antichrist going to come from?" Although there are several theories, I believe the book of Daniel is very specific on the origin of the Antichrist.

When considering the primary prophetic books of the Bible, Daniel is considered to be a strong book of prophecy to the nations. In contrast, the book of Zechariah is considered prophecy to the Jews, and the book of Revelation to the church. All three books intermingle, but Daniel's dominant focus is the nations, so we're going to look at Daniel to discover the future of the nations and find out the Antichrist's origin.

DANIEL'S PROPHETIC DREAM

After Nebuchadnezzar's dream, Daniel also dreamed a prophetic dream. His dream coincided with the message of King Nebuchadnezzar's dream, only Daniel saw animals instead of the figure of metals.

> And four great beasts came up from the sea, diverse one from another.
>
> The first was like a lion, and had eagle's wings: I beheld till the wings thereof were plucked, and it was lifted up from the earth, and made stand upon the feet as a man, and a man's heart was given to it.
>
> And behold another beast, a second, like to a bear, and it raised up itself on one side, and it had three ribs in the mouth of it between the teeth of it: and they said thus unto it, Arise, devour much flesh.

After this I beheld, and lo another, like a leopard, which had upon the back of it four wings of a fowl; the beast had also four heads; and dominion was given to it.

After this I saw in the night visions, and behold a fourth beast, dreadful and terrible, and strong exceedingly; and it had great iron teeth: it devoured and brake in pieces, and stamped the residue with the feet of it: and it was diverse from all the beasts that were before it; and it had ten horns.

I considered the horns, and, behold, there came up among them another little horn, before whom there were three of the first horns plucked up by the roots: and, behold, in this horn were eyes like the eyes of man, and a mouth speaking great things.

Daniel 7:3-8

What animals did Daniel see in this passage? He saw a golden-headed lion (Babylonians), a bear (Medes-Persians), a leopard (Greeks), and a fierce-looking iron creature (Romans). These animals are important to us because we're going to see them again in Revelation 17 when we study the end-time prophecy revealed in that chapter.

Previously I mentioned that out of the ten-toed kingdom (the revival of the Roman Empire) a horn will sprout out. This indicates that the Antichrist will come from the area of the "fourth beast, dreadful and terrible," the Old Roman Empire. This is Europe, particularly the area around the Mediterranean. History tells that the Roman Empire died down for an extended period. However, this prophecy reveals that it will sprout up again in ten countries. Out of the ten countries that rise again, a little horn will arise that will be the Antichrist.

From the context of Daniel's visions, we know that the Antichrist is going to rise up and fight three of the smaller countries in this group. He will take them over just as the little horn will overtake the others. Because he has great power to make war, after he conquers three of those ten major countries, the other seven will join him. In addition, much of the Antichrist's activities will take place in this area of the world—the Old Roman Empire.

After God gave Daniel this dream, He gave him a second pondering vision. This time, the dream narrowed down to two animals, or nations—a ram and a he-goat.

> Then I lifted up mine eyes, and saw, and, behold, there stood before the river a ram which had two horns: and the two horns were high; but one was higher than the other, and the higher came up last.
>
> I saw the ram pushing westward, and northward, and southward; so that no beasts might stand before him, neither was there any that could deliver out of his hand; but he did according to his will, and became great.
>
> And as I was considering, behold, an he goat came from the west on the face of the whole earth, and touched not the ground: and the goat had a notable horn between his eyes.
>
> And he came to the ram that had two horns, which I had seen standing before the river, and ran unto him in the fury of his power.

And I saw him come close unto the ram, and he was moved with choler against him, and smote the ram, and brake his two horns: and there was no power in the ram to stand before him, but he cast him down to the ground, and stamped upon him: and there was none that could deliver the ram out of his hand.

Therefore the he goat waxed very great: and when he was strong, the great horn was broken; and for it came up four notable ones toward the four winds of heaven.

And out of one of them came forth a little horn, which waxed exceeding great, toward the south, and toward the east, and toward the pleasant land.

Daniel 8:3-9

In this dream the ram hits the he-goat, but the he-goat conquers him. The ram represents the Medo-Persian Empire. In biblical times a ram was the symbol of the Persians and had two horns or two kingdoms, namely Media and Persia.[7] The he-goat represents the Greek Empire. A goat was a very proper symbol of the Greek or Macedonian people; in fact, two hundred years before the time of Daniel they were known as the goats' people.[8]

From the he-goat's head stems a great horn. This great horn is the first Greek leader; most scholars agree that it is Alexander the Great.[9] Suddenly, this great horn breaks off the he-goat and four notable horns spring forth. I believe these four horns represent Syria, Medo-Persia, Turkey, and Palestine.

Finally, from those four horns a smaller horn arises. Remember, this horn is the Antichrist. Interestingly, this small horn (or Antichrist) makes war with the south, east, and west. The south encompasses the area of Egypt, the east includes Palestine, and the west comprises Medo-Persia. The Antichrist does not make war with the north (Syria). Could this suggest that he is from the north, or from the area of Syria?

Daniel's second vision pinpoints the location of the Antichrist's origin even more so. Syria is part of the Old Roman Empire. Additionally, the Antichrist is the head of the northern army, which is referred to in Joel 2:20.

> But I will remove far off from you the northern army, and will drive him into a land barren and desolate, with his face coward the east sea, and his hinder part toward the utmost sea, and his stink shall come up, and his ill savour shall come up, because he hath done great things.

He is called the king of Babylon in Isaiah 14:4 and the Assyrian in Isaiah 10:5. These Scriptures seem to point to the fact that the Antichrist comes from a country that is near the Black and Caspian seas, was part of the former Babylonian and Assyrian empires, and is north of Israel. Again, these indicators seem to point to the area of Syria. Let's look at one more Bible passage on this.

AT THE END OF TIME

The Antichrist is alluded to in Daniel 11:21-39, which discusses Antiochus Epiphanes (remember him?). We saw earlier that Antiochus is the Syrian king who is considered a prototype of the Antichrist and his future dealings with the nation of Israel. Daniel 11 is considered by many to be a chapter of predominantly fulfilled prophecy. In one sense this is true. Daniel's prophecy in verses 1-39 was fulfilled in history by Antiochus; but events that will take place "at the time of the end" are yet to come, as in verses 40-45 TLB:

> "Then at the time of the end, the king of the south will attack him again, and the northern king will react with the strength and fury of a whirlwind; his vast army and navy will rush out to bury him with their might.
>
> He will invade various lands on the way, including Israel, the Pleasant Land, and overthrow the governments of many nations. Moab, Edom, and most of Ammon will escape, but Egypt and many other lands will be occupied.
>
> He will capture all the treasures of Egypt, and the Libyans and Ethiopians shall be his servants.
>
> "But then news from the east and north will alarm him, and he will return in great anger to destroy as he goes.
>
> He will halt between Jerusalem and the sea and there pitch his royal tents, but while he is there his time will suddenly run out, and there will be no one to help him."

We're beginning to put the pieces to the end-times "puzzle" together with everything we've been looking at so far. I believe that it will cause your spiritual confidence and peace to dramatically increase as your understanding of end-time prophecy increases. As we go deeper into the Scriptures on the last days, we're going to continue to look at this major end-time personality. God put the Antichrist in His Word because He wanted us to know all about him.

CHAPTER 7

WHAT WILL THE ANTICHRIST DO?

So far we have an idea of where the Antichrist will come from—possibly around the Mediterranean area. We know what he'll look like—mean eyes, big mouth, "ugly" face. Remember how he'll talk? At first, he will have smooth words that drip with honey. He'll be a great deceiver. And he'll be very smart. In this chapter, we're going to see what he can do and how his character and his actions all flow together.

Basically there are two kinds of rulers (I'm talking about the evil rulers who lust for power). Religious rulers who want to rule over people, as happened with David Koresh and the Branch Davidian religious sect in Waco, Texas, in 1999, and with Jim Jones and his Jonestown cult in the 1970s, both of which ended in tragedy. Religious rulers like that want to rule over people's souls; they want to own people. Then there's another kind of ruler who wants to rule the world and be involved in major commerce and land development .

The Antichrist will be both kinds of rulers. He will want to rule the world and be worshiped as a god, and he will want to be the major "player" in commercial endeavors. At some point he will rise up and be very powerful and very strong in war. During that time of great distress, or the Great Tribulation, he'll also be very experienced in commerce and making money.

> Lo, this is the man that made not God his strength; but trusted in the *abundance of his riches,* and strengthened himself in his wickedness.
>
> Psalms 52:7

One way he will make money is by raising taxes. In Daniel 11 the angel explained Daniel's vision to him. In the explanation, the angel described the work of the Antichrist as a tax raiser.

> Then shall stand up in his estate a *raiser of taxes* in the glory of the kingdom: but within few days he shall be destroyed, neither in anger, nor in battle.
>
> Daniel 11:20

While this verse is referring to Antiochus, whom we saw earlier, it also represents the Antichrist and what he will do in the last days.[1] I'm going to stir up your memory for a moment in reference to the Antichrist being a powerful moneymaker.

Earlier when we were going through the rooms in the "house" of Revelation, we saw two Bible chapters in the fifth room, or the satanic room— Revelation 17 and 18 (see Figure 4.1). These two chapters speak figuratively of two Babylons.

The first Babylon is ecclesiastical (church; religious). The ecclesiastical Babylon is the church system the Antichrist will build and of which he will declare himself god.

The second Babylon is commercial. The Antichrist is going to build a tremendous commercial center on the base of ancient Babylon. That is what Daniel 8:25 means when it states "...he shall cause craft to prosper...." From Scripture, we know that this commercial Babylon will be very prosperous. For example, the following passage tells us that when Babylon does finally fall, all the merchants weep and cry.

And he cried mightily with a strong voice, saying, Babylon the great is fallen, is fallen....

And the merchants of the earth shall weep and mourn over her; for no man buyeth their merchandise any more:

The merchandise of gold, and silver, and precious stones, and of pearls, and fine linen, and purple, and silk, and scarlet, and all thyine wood, and all manner vessels of ivory, and all manner vessels of most precious wood, and of brass, and iron, and marble,

And cinnamon, and odours, and ointments, and frankincense, and wine, and oil, and fine flour, and wheat, and beasts, and sheep, and horses, and chariots, and slaves, and souls of men.

And the fruits chat thy soul lusted after are departed from thee, and all things which were dainty and goodly are departed from thee, and thou shalt find them no more at all.

The merchants of these things, which were made rich by her, shall stand afar off for the fear of her torment, weeping and wailing....

And cried when they saw the smoke of her burning, saying, What city is like unto this great city!

And they cast dust on their heads, and cried, weeping and wailing, saying, Alas, alas, that great city, wherein were made rich all that had ships in the sea by reason of her costliness! for in one hour is she made desolate.

Revelation 18:2,11-15,18,19

These merchants are really sad! For this much weeping, the Antichrist surely will build a mighty, powerful, and prosperous commercial Babylon. This passage truly fits right in with Daniel 8:25.

DECEIVE, DECEIVE, DECEIVE

After the Antichrist's war, he gets himself up in a high position by using his major tool—deception. I covered deception earlier in this book, but remember, the Bible says that his method of deception is so effective that even the elect (believers) could be deceived.

For there shall arise false Christs, and false prophets, and shall shew great signs and wonders; insomuch that, if it were possible, they shall deceive the very elect.

Matthew 24:24

We will not be deceived if we cling to the Word, saturate ourselves with it, and understand end-time prophecy. That is our key to victory in these last days.

DECLARE PEACE

After the Antichrist enters the scene, makes war, and conquers nations, he will usher in peace. According to Paul, when the Antichrist comes on the scene in a position of power, he will deceive people worldwide into thinking it is a time of peace and safety, but "...then sudden destruction cometh upon them, as travail upon a woman with child; and they shall not escape" (1 Thess. 5:3).

The Antichrist will say something like, "I'm here to make peace," and he will persuade the whole world to follow him because he has become the great giver of peace.

During this peacetime he will accomplish something that will appear to be miraculous. He will solve the Israeli/Arab conflict by creating peace between them. This will be covered more later on, but it will amaze and astound many and cause the Jews to enter into a (temporary) covenant with him, thinking that he is their long-awaited Messiah.

Unfortunately, the peace the Antichrist will offer will be a false and temporary peace. It will only last for a short time.

ESTABLISH A FALSE RELIGIOUS SYSTEM

Even though the Antichrist will gather the entire world to follow him, his hunger for glory will continue to increase. This is the same sin that caused Satan to be exiled from heaven.[2] In an attempt to satisfy this hunger, the Antichrist will establish a whole false church system designed to bring worship to him.

> **And there came one of the seven angels which had the seven vials, and talked with me, saying unto me, Come**

hither; I will shew unto thee the judgment of the great whore that sitteth upon many waters.

Revelation 17:1

According to *The Wycliffe Bible Commentary*, the "great whore" mentioned here represents the false religious system of the Antichrist: "...She is definitely some vast spiritual system that persecutes the saints of God, betraying that to which she was called. She enters into relations with the governments of this earth, and for a while rules them. I think the closest we can come to an identification is to understand this harlot as symbolic of a vast spiritual power arising at the end of the age, which enters into a league with the world and compromises with wordly forces. Instead of being spiritually true, she is spiritually false, and thus exercises an evil influence in the name of religion."[3]

In Revelation 17:1 this harlot, "the great whore," is seen sitting upon "many waters," which means that she has many people under her power. Verse 2 details explicitly nations following this mass false religion.

With whom the kings of the earth have committed fornication, and the inhabitants of the earth have been made drunk with the wine of her fornication.

In the next Scripture, the "whore" sits upon a "scarlet beast." Remember, earlier we established that one of the Antichrist's many names is beast. When we see the woman in this passage, she appears very rich. Arrayed in purple and scarlet color, adorned with gold, precious stones, and pearls, the woman pictures a wealthy false church.

> So he carried me away in the spirit into the wilderness:
> and I saw a woman sit upon a scarlet coloured beast, full
> of names of blasphemy, having seven heads and ten horns.
>
> Revelation 17:3

The reference to the "ten horns" represents the ten king-doms that the Antichrist will unite. You will remember these also pictured as "ten toes" in Nebuchadnezzar's dream. The beast enters again with the seven heads and ten horns, which conveys that these ten kingdoms will be subdued under him. What are the "seven heads?"

This false religious system did not start with the Anti-christ. This system's roots trace back to the story of Cain and Abel when Cain tried to offer his own works to God instead of a blood sacrifice.[4]

Throughout history, this false religious system is exposed through stories like Nimrod and the tower of Babel. In the Old Testament, many of the kings practiced idolatry, the Egyptians worshiped the Nile River (among other things), and the Canaanites participated in satanism. The false church will sit on top of the end-time nations. Historically, the false church began with the building of Babel by Nimrod. It started in sin.

> And Cush begat Nimrod: he began to be a mighty one in
> the earth.
>
> He was a mighty hunter before the Lord: wherefore it is
> said, Even as Nimrod the mighty hunter before the Lord.
>
> And the beginning of his kingdom was Babel, and Erech,
> and Accad, and Calneh, in the land of Shinar.
>
> Genesis 10:8-10

The purpose for building the tower of Babel was to make a name for the builders. They tried to begin a new and idolatrous religion. The word *Babel* has several meanings, including "confusion" and "gate of god...."[5] When the builders attempted to reach heaven via their tower, God confused their tongues and scattered them. These builders fit the description that Paul referred to in the book of Romans:

> Because that, when they knew God, they glorified *him* not as God, neither were thankful; but became vain in their imaginations, and their foolish heart was darkened.
>
> Professing themselves to be wise, they became fools,
>
> And changed the glory of the uncorruptible God into an image made like to corruptible man, and to birds, and fourfooted beasts, and creeping things.
>
> And even as they did not like to retain God in *their* knowledge, God gave them over to a reprobate mind, to do those things which are not convenient.
>
> Romans 1:21-23,28

False religion was the reason that God called Abraham out of the Babylonian area. Idolatry was common there.

> And Joshua said unto all the people, Thus saith the Lord God of Israel, Your fathers dwelt on the other side of the flood in old time, even Terah, the father of Abraham, and the father of
>
> Nachor: *and they served other gods.*
>
> Joshua 24:2

God desired to establish Abraham as a holy nation, one that only worshiped Him, and He knew that this idol worship would eventually affect Abraham if he didn't leave. Matthew Henry wrote, "...His [Abraham's] country had become idolatrous, his kindred and his father's house were a constant temptation to him, and he could not continue with them without danger of being infected by them .... "[6]

The seriousness of practicing Satan's false religion can be seen in the story of Achan. After the Israelites victory at Jericho, he stole a Babylonian garment and some silver and gold (spoils of war that the Bible calls "the accursed thing") in disobedience to Joshua's command.[7] Achan paid a heavy price for his actions—he was stoned to death.

> And Achan answered Joshua, and said, Indeed I have sinned against the Lord God of Israel, and thus and thus have I done:
>
> When I saw among the spoils a goodly Babylonish garment, and two hundred shekels of silver, and a wedge of gold of fifty shekels weight, then I covered them, and took them; and, behold, they are hid in the earth in the midst of my tent, and the silver under it.
>
> And Joshua said, Why hast thou troubled us? the Lord shall trouble thee this day. And all Israel stoned him with stones, and burned them with fire, after they had stoned them with stones.
>
> Joshua 7:20,21,25

The Israelites placed a high level of seriousness on false religions. They knew that idol worship is a serious sin against

God. Why shouldn't they? Because Israel had often fallen into idolatry, even after ages of warnings against this practice by the Old Testament prophets, the Israelites were carried away to Babylon.[8] During their captivity, Nebuchadnezzar made a golden image to worship,[9] and his grandson profaned the vessels of God's house. Eventually, Babylon was judged and passed into the hands of Darius the Mede.

The term "MYSTERY, BABYLON" from Revelation 17:5 represents false religion, which has been around through the ages:

"And upon her [the great whore's] forehead was a name written, MYSTERY, BABYLON THE GREAT, THE MOTHER OF HARLOTS AND ABOMINATIONS OF THE EARTH." It is Satan's substitute for true Christianity. Anything that is against the blood sacrifice—against the Father's way of redemption through Jesus Christ—is cultish.

False religion has always competed with the truth of God, but in the Antichrist's reign, it will come to a head.

CREATE AN ABOMINATION

After making war, the Antichrist will establish the "abomination of desolation." The Bible mentions this three times in the book of Daniel.

> And he shall confirm the covenant with many for one week: and in the midst of the week he shall cause the sacrifice and the oblation to cease, and for the overspreading of *abominations he shall make it desolate,* even until the consummation, and that determined shall be poured upon the desolate.
>
> Daniel 9:27

> And arms shall stand on his part, and they shall pollute
> the sanctuary of strength, and shall take away the daily
> sacrifice, and they shall place the *abomination that*
> *maketh desolate.*
>
> Daniel 11:31

> And from the time that the daily sacrifice shall be taken
> away, and the *abomination that maketh desolate* set up,
> there shall be a thousand two hundred and ninety days.
>
> Daniel 12:11

Daniel 11:31 prophesied that Antiochus Epiphanes, a type or shadow of the Antichrist, would build an altar to Zeus in the temple. This is called the "abomination that causes desolation" (NIV translation), a desecration of the altar which destroyed its true purpose. Similarly, the Antichrist will establish an abomination, or demonic counterfeit worship, in the sanctuary.[10]

SET HIMSELF UP AS AN IDOL

It will nor be enough for the Antichrist to have a universal religion and united world under his control. His hunger for power will cause him to promote himself as a god demanding worship. He will do something inconceivable—he will build an idol of himself in the Holy of Holies of the temple. Incredibly, that idol will begin to speak and many will be amazed. However, one particular group that will not be amazed are the Jews. Through this forced idol worship, they will realize that this Antichrist cannot be their promised Messiah. Idol worship contradicts everything their Lord Jehovah has established. This will cause the Jewish people to turn against the Antichrist.

In this time period, the Antichrist is killed. However, he somehow arises from the dead, completing Revelation 17:11 that says, "The beast that was, and is not, even he is...." This verse means that the beast "was" alive, then "is not" alive, and then "he is" alive again.

Why does he do this? What is the purpose? His goal, as always, is to counterfeit Christ! Jesus died, rose again, and now reigns. So the Antichrist's ulterior motive in completing this feat will be to confuse people into following him as the one true god.

CAUSE THE JEWS TO RETURN TO GOD

When the Antichrist sets himself as an idol in the temple of Jerusalem, it will drive the Jews to consider that this is wrong. They will realize that he is falsely personifying the long awaited Messiah and has committed an abomination (the abomination of desolation) by setting himself as a false idol in the Holy of Holies. As it becomes clear to the Jews that they have been serving the wrong master, they will turn away from him, rebelling against his leadership, and begin to turn back to God.

The Antichrist, however, will become enraged and will turn his fury towards them. He will begin to lead a major campaign against the Jews and their Promised Land. This is another aspiration of the Antichrist's leadership: to control the Promised Land—Israel.

Remembering the atrocities of the past, scores of Jews will begin to return to their homeland of Israel.

During this time of the Tribulation, a great revival will break out among the Jewish people. Many will repent and be "sealed" by God for evangelizing the world—144,000 according to the Bible. These same Jews are responsible for turning great numbers of the Jewish people back to God. In the end, many Jews will lead all of heaven in wonderful praises to the Lamb.[11]

CONTROL "THE PLEASANT LAND"

You may be wondering why everyone wants the Promised Land. After much study I discovered an area of politics called geopolitics that I believe has much to do with the desire of various nations to gain control of this area of the world.

Geo is associated with the earth. *Politics* is the art or science of conducting governments. *Geopolitics* is defined as "**1**: a study of the influence of such factors as geography, economics, and demography on the politics and especially the foreign policy of a state; **2**: a governmental policy guided by geopolitics; **3**: a combination of political and geographic factors relating to something (as a state or particular resources)."[12] Basically, we could say that geopolitics is the art of governing the earth, or segments of the earth.

With that in mind, I believe that the geopolitics of the end times has three basic premises:

1. He who rules Eastern Europe commands the heartland (the Middle East).
2. He who rules the heartland commands the world island (Palestine).

3.   He who rules the world island commands the world.

The geopolitics of this region teaches that if anyone can truly rule Palestine, he can command the world. Thus, he who rules Europe controls the Middle East, commands Palestine, and reigns over the world. It seems obvious that this principle is the reason for the international hunger to control the Middle East. The Antichrist is no exception to the temptation. He will desire to manage the Promised Land. Daniel predicted this thousands of years before.

> **And out of one of them came forth a little horn, which waxed exceeding great, toward the south, and toward the east, and toward the *pleasant land*.**
>
> **Daniel 8:9**

The words "pleasant land" in the above passage represent the Holy Land, or Israel. The original Hebrew word for *pleasant* in this verse is *tsebiy*, which means "splendor, beauty, or beautiful."[13] The land of the Israelites has often been described in this way—a land of beauty, a land flowing with milk and honey. It is not surprising that Daniel, who was in exile from his beloved country, used this term to describe it.

DECLARE WAR

As the Antichrist gains popularity among the world, he will begin to counsel with the nations and secure a temporary peace. His hunger for power will drive him to desire more than simply being the counselor to the world; he will want to own the world.

The Antichrist will begin to raise himself up. This coincides with the four seals we read about in Revelation. These seals all lead to the returning of Christ.

The red horse is spoken about in Revelation 6 when referring to war. In the same chapter of Revelation as the red horse of war, another horse is mentioned—the pale horse representing death. As the Antichrist rises up in power, he will cause war, which will lead to great death and martyrdom upon the earth. He will do this by stirring up the international political arena.

Eventually, the Jews' return to Jehovah will enrage the Antichrist, and he will decide to extinguish the Jews for the last time. So he will rally all the nations of the world against Israel, and they will march from the valley of Megiddo to Jerusalem. Thus, the Antichrist will declare the greatest war of all time—Armageddon.

DRAW THE NATIONS TO FIGHT

Among other catastrophes, the Antichrist remains in leadership. During the last few years of the Tribulation, various events (including the Jews' return to God) will cause the Antichrist's fury to increase. His fury will motivate him to unite the nations in league with him to gather for the greatest war of all time. The nations will gather in the valley of Megiddo to attack the nation of Israel.

Three spirits will be released during the last half of the Tribulation, which will motivate the Antichrist to take this action.

> And I saw *three unclean spirits* like frogs *come* out of the mouth of the dragon, and out of the mouth of the beast, and out of the mouth of the false prophet.
>
> For they are the spirits of devils, working miracles, which go forth unto the kings of the earth and of the whole world, to gather them to the battle of that great day of God Almighty.
>
> Revelation 16:13,14

The prophet Ezekiel explained in his prophecies of the end times that the three spirits of Revelation 16:13 are sent out to gather the kings of (1) Meshech and Tubal; (2) Persia, Ethiopia, and Libya; and (3) Gomer and Togarmah.[14]

Meshech and Tubal

We have already seen that originally Meshech and Tubal were not the names of countries, but sons of Japheth, Noah's son. God showed Ezekiel that the nations would constantly change over the centuries, so He called the areas by the names of Noah's descendants who settled there.

Japheth became the father of the Caucasian people.[15] Historical records show that Meshech and Tubal (Russian and Slavic peoples) settled near the Black and Caspian seas. These bodies of water are currently bounded by Turkey, Romania, Bulgaria, the Ukraine, Iran, and former Soviet southern republics such as Georgia, Azerbaijan, and Kazakhstan.

Persia, Ethiopia, and Libya

Today, Ethiopia and Libya are the same nations that they were during Ezekiel's time, but much smaller. Persia reached from modern day India to Greece, encompassing what is now Iran and part of Afghanistan. During the end times these countries will grow in might, power, and size. This is not only possible but is highly probable because each country sits on reserves of oil, natural gas, and other minerals.

For example, Ethiopia has left its natural resources untapped for decades. Ethiopia, which is now poor and reliant on other countries for financial and military aid, will become a major world power because the world will turn to her for resources.

Gomer and Togarmah

Gomer, the son of Japheth, and Togarmah, Japheth's grandson, settled farther west and north in Europe. Their descendants now live in several countries, including Austria, Italy, France, Sweden, Germany, and the former Yugoslavia.

The kings of these three federations will be part of the Antichrist's confederate nations and will have the biggest armed forces. Because they will doubt the Antichrist, he will have to lure them into action by using the supernatural powers of the three unclean spirits. Although the Antichrist's other allied nations will be part of this army that converges on Israel at Armageddon, Ezekiel's three countries will be the major forces.

THE ANTICHRIST'S CONFEDERACY

Since national boundaries and forms of government change often, I would probably be wrong within a year if I gave the current names of the countries that will be a part of the Antichrist's confederacy. For instance, what was Yugoslavia became Bosnia-Herzegovina, Serbia, Croatia, Slovenia, Macedonia, and others in 1992. West and East Germany were reunited as one nation in 1990. Additionally in 1991, the Soviet Union broke off into more than a dozen independent states.

What I can say is that the Antichrist's confederacy of ten nations (whether they are ten nations we can recognize today or ten new nations) will come out of the area surrounding the Mediterranean Sea, covering Europe, the Middle East, and northern Africa.

Remember, Daniel's prophecies provide this information. To summarize them:

Nebuchadnezzar's dream of an image with a golden head, silver arms and chest, brass stomach and thighs, iron legs, and feet of iron and clay, was the same as Daniel's dream of four beasts, a lion, bear, leopard, and iron image that had ten horns.[16]

The gold head/lion represents Babylon; the silver arms and chest/bear represent the Medo-Persians; the brass stomach and thighs/leopard represent Greece; the iron legs/iron image represent Rome; and the iron and clay toes/ten horns represent the Antichrist's kingdom.

These visions correspond with the beast of Revelation 13, which is described as having seven heads and ten horns that are each crowned. They also correspond with the beast of Revelation 17, which is described as having seven heads and ten horns. This beast is the Antichrist.

John explains in this last book of the Bible that the beast's seven heads, "...are seven kings: five are fallen, one is, and the other is not yet come; and when he cometh, he must continue a short space" (Rev. 17:10). The seven kingdoms are those that afflicted the Jews when they were a nation. So, the first five kings are Egypt, Assyria, Babylon, the Medo-Persians, and Greece. The one that "is" in John's day was Rome. And the one that is yet to come and will "continue a short space" is the Antichrist.

The ten horns represent the ten countries that ally with the Antichrist. They come out of the boundaries of these seven kingdoms.

WILL AMERICA JOIN THE ANTICHRIST?

Will America be a part of the Antichrist's confederacy and end-time army? No, the Antichrist does not conquer the whole world, only the part of the world that was once the Roman Empire. America was not part of any of the seven world empires that afflicted Israel.

America, the countries that were once part of the British Empire, and various other nations will revolt against the Antichrist as he becomes more aggressive against Israel. Ezekiel calls these countries, "Sheba, and Dedan, and the merchants of Tarshish, with all the young lions thereof..." (Ezek. 38:13). Again, Ezekiel uses the descendants of Noah to describe the nations.

Dedan and Sheba are both descendants of Ham. Dedan's people settled on the northwest shores of the Persian Gulf, including northern Saudi Arabia and Kuwait.[17] Sheba and his family settled on the southwest shores of the Persian Gulf. This area includes southern Saudi Arabia, Oman, and the United Arab Emirates. Today the peoples of Sheba and

Dedan consist mostly of Arabs and are generally considered to be enemies of Israel. However, when the Antichrist creates a peace treaty between the Arabs and Israel, these countries will keep their word and protect Israel.

Tarshish was Noah's great-grandson who settled in the western Mediterranean Sea near the Rock of Gibraltar in Spain.[18] The merchants of Tarshish were famous for their ships, and their homes were considered the farthest point in the world. Because Tarshish was as far away as one could possibly go at that time (which is shown by Jonah's attempt to flee there when he was running away from God), it represented a distant but unknown land. This land will have a worldwide influence in the last days. The "young lions" are offshoots of that country or commonwealth.[19]

Although Tarshish was in what is now Spain and the Spanish Empire had many branches, I believe God is referring to Great Britain and her former colonies. These countries, including the United States, have greater worldwide influence than the former Spanish colonies. However, even if the prophecy did refer to Spain, many parts of the United States were originally part of the former Spanish Empire. Therefore, they would be part of the armies that revolt against the Antichrist.

THE ULTIMATE VICTORY

Although the Antichrist's leadership will create horrible conditions upon the earth, God can, and will, transform these actions into a good result.

This aspect of God's personality is seen in the story of Joseph being sold into slavery by his brothers. After Joseph was sent into Egypt, God opened doors of promotion to him. Later, when Joseph reunited with his brothers, he told them, "As for you, you meant evil against me, but God meant it for good in order to bring about this present result, to preserve many people alive" (Gen. 50:20 ASB).

In the same way, God will ultimately have the victory over the Antichrist's deeds. One of His major victories will be fulfilling the covenant He made with His chosen people—the Jews.

BRIGHT AND BLEAK FUTURE

Although the Antichrist seemingly accomplishes great feats during his time of leadership on earth, God, in His infinite wisdom, inspired the ancient Bible prophecies we study today. That means that God knew and preplanned the end times even before we were born. While He does not cause the Antichrist's rise to power, He does allow this rise and ultimately utilizes Satan's tool for His plan. God allows the false "christ's" evil ways to contrast Jesus' love for mankind in the eyes of the whole world. Ultimately, many will turn to the one true Messiah—Jesus Christ.

What does the future hold for the Antichrist? God's final plan for him includes total annihilation. In Revelation 19:20 we see that the beast and the false prophet will be taken and cast into the lake of fire. Unfortunately, there is no salvation for those people who took his mark—the deceived. Verse 21 records what will come to pass—they will be "slain by the sword of him that sat upon the horse, which sword proceeded out of his mouth: and all the fowls were filled with their flesh." At this point Jesus' victory will be complete.

So far, we've seen some of the things that will help make the way for the Antichrist to come and what he does once he's here and in power. But that is only one side of the story. This present world is going to end and a new day is coming, one in which the prince of the power of the air[20] will be destroyed, and the Prince of Peace will set up His kingdom and reign for all eternity.

CHAPTER 8

WHY ALL SIXES?

> ...and his number is Six hundred threescore and six.
>
> Revelation 13:18

Many people who know nothing else about the end times have heard of the number "666." People wonder what it stands for. Why all sixes? What will it be used for? I've heard some very interesting explanations for this number, but the Bible gives the true meaning.

In the book of Revelation, six represents several things. According to Revelation 13:16-18, it represents an evil number or satanic number ("the number of the beast"), and it represents "the number of a man." Man was created on the sixth day (Gen. 1:26,31), and in Matthew 16:23, Jesus said that Satan is man centered, that he thinks as people think.

Three (the amount of numerals in the number 666) represents trinity. *The Wycliffe Bible Commentary* calls 666 "the trinity of six." I too believe that the use of three six's is Satan's sign for his unholy trinity. It's no surprise that his mark in the end times will be "666."

In biblical times the method was practiced of representing numbers in words, names, and phrases by letters of the alphabet. With that in mind, it is probable that the Greek name of the beast will contain the number 666. For people who receive Jesus as their Savior after the Rapture, this will help them to determine who the Antichrist is.

The fact that no one will be able to buy or sell without receiving this mark is often emphasized over other aspects of 666, but that is not the mark's main purpose. One of Satan's primary purposes for writing his mark on his followers is that it's a counterfeit of God. Remember, Satan's ultimate goal and ambition is to "be like the most High" (Isa. 14:14).

Satan likes to mimic the works of God. God has a Son, so Satan has a "son" (the Antichrist). God has a system of worship, so Satan has a system of worship. God manifests Himself in the form of a Trinity, so Satan has an unholy trinity. God has set a seal, or mark, on His people, and so does Satan.

Several Hebrew words for *mark* are used in Scripture. One of those words, *tav*, means "a sign"[2] and was used by the prophet Ezekiel in Ezekiel 9:4,6, which told of his vision of the destruction of the wicked. Those sealed on their foreheads with the seal, or mark, of the living God would be kept from harm and protected in the same way that the blood of a lamb was sprinkled on the doorposts of the homes of the Israelites. (Ex. 12:22,23.)[3]

Satan's attempts to counterfeit God will come to a head when he sets a mark on his "children" or followers to be like God. This is evident in the New Testament use of the word *mark*. The Greek meaning of this word in Revelation 13:16-17 (which refers to the mark of the beast) is *charagma*, meaning "a stamp" or "imprinted mark." According to Scripture this mark, in some form of the number 666, will be the badge of the followers of the Antichrist and will be stamped on their forehead or their right hand.[4]

In the same way that owners of cattle brand and mark their stock, the people who take the mark of the beast will be branded under the Antichrist. Taking this mark upon their foreheads or hands will actually be the sign and seal that they belong to the devil and his henchmen.

Opinions differ on whether or not the mark of the beast is an actual mark or is symbolic in some way. But the reality is that while those who do not take this mark will suffer deadly consequences on earth, the fate of those with the mark will be much worse.

> Then a third angel followed them shouting, "Anyone worshiping the Creature from the sea and his statue, and accepting his mark on the forehead or the hand
>
> must drink the wine of the anger of God; it is poured out undiluted into God's cup of wrath. And they will be tormented with fire and burning sulphur in the presence of the holy angels and the Lamb.
>
> The smoke of their torture rises forever and ever, and they will have no relief day or night, for they have worshiped the Creature and his statue, and have been tattooed with the code of his name.
>
> Revelation 14:9-11 TLB

In the well-known exposition on Revelation by Bible scholar Joseph Seiss, he described the fate of those who take the mark as helpless slaves and cattle who submit themselves to the devil's branding iron, "and yielding, to perish everlastingly, for there is no more salvation for anyone upon whom is this 'mark....'" [5]

Those who take the mark of the beast will not be simply receiving a mark; it will not really be about buying and selling. This passage reveals that it will be much more serious than that because whoever receives the mark will be worshiping the beast and rejecting God. That is the most important aspect of 666.

THE FALSE PROPHET

And he had power to give life unto the image of the beast, that the image of the beast should both speak, and cause that as many as would not worship the image of the beast should be killed.

Revelation 13:15

What will living conditions be like when taking the mark will be enforced? During the Tribulation Satan will introduce a new evil character, the third member of his unholy trinity, the False Prophet. This second beast will arrive on the scene with the power to do signs and wonders. Remember, he will cause people to worship the Antichrist and make a talking idol of the beast, which he will place in the temple. The False Prophet will order the death of anyone who refuses to worship the Antichrist. In fact, he will lead many people of the world to worship him by controlling the wealth.

Israel will lose its spiritual protection when it temporarily makes an alliance with the devil, so it will be powerless to stop the assault of the False Prophet and the Antichrist.

From all of the death and famine in the world during the end times, Israel's economy and agriculture will fail.

> Lament like a virgin girded with sackcloth for the husband of her youth.
>
> The meat offering and the drink offering is cut off from the house of the Lord; the priests, the Lord's ministers, mourn.
>
> The field is wasted, the land mourneth; for the corn is wasted: the new wine is dried up, the oil languisheth.
>
> Joel 1:8-10

The Antichrist will strip the country of all its other valuables. The prophet Joel gave a picture of this destruction in Joel 1:4, saying that it will be like the palmerworm, locust, canker worm, and caterpillar invasions of ancient days, when each new bug eats a part of the crops until even the seeds are gone.

From this economic failure, the Antichrist will seize the opportunity to force the world to follow his system. Instituting an international embargo on food, goods, and staples, the Anitchrist will attempt to "starve out" rebels against his cause. Therefore, no one will be allowed to buy or sell unless they do it within the Antichrist's system, which is pictured in Revelation 6:5 as the black horseman who is released by the opening of the third seal. Basically, the Antichrist will control the world with his mark.

You may be thinking, *That is out of the question*. But as one Bible scholar says, controlling the world may not be as impossible as it sounds: "When you combine political power with economic power and all religion, you have a formula for controlling the whole world. But the lost world worships money and power, so the task will not be too difficult. "[6]

MARK-OF-THE-BEAST TECHNOLOGY

Many systems are currently in place that would make control of world trade possible. Computers, cable systems, microchips, and transportation are advancing quickly. Computer chips have been invented which, when inserted under the skin, can carry a person's vital information, such as name, address, credit history, banking information, employment, medical records, and so forth.

Our governments are also relying more and more on a one-world trade system. All of Europe and the three countries of North America are working jointly to bolster their economies.

I'm not trying to say that any of these will be the technology from which the mark will come. Right now no one knows what the Antichrist will use. I believe that all of this is a foreshadow of events in Revelation 13 and will allow the Antichrist to take over easily and manage a worldwide economy.

From present-day world conditions and the picture the Scriptures paint of the end times, it seems likely that the time will shortly come for these events to take place. Revelation 13:6 says that it's wisdom to understand about the number of the name of the future Antichrist. The wisdom we need is not so much to try to figure out what his name will be.

Remember, we will be taken up in the Rapture before the Antichrist is revealed. We need wisdom now to detect and discern the signs of the times through the bad principles of the antichrist spirit that is at work in the world today.

There are people who do not know, or who refuse, Jesus. They will most likely become victims to the lies and deceits of the devil.

Yet God in His mercy has shown ahead of time in His Word where their unbelief is leading them so that they can learn and change before it's too late. We as believers need to get the message out before the Rapture comes. People who reject God's Son Jesus are opening their souls to the devil's "messiah," the Antichrist.

Part of being a "watcher" is to bring into the kingdom as many souls as we can *now*. No one should have to suffer at the hands of Satan's evil accomplices. We see many instances in the Bible where God has protected His people from harm. Christ's work on the cross was the ultimate example of this protection—Jesus paid the price for our sins so we might not die in our iniquity. He shed His blood so ours would not have to flow.

CHAPTER 9

A "CHAT" WITH THE ENEMY

The biggest reason that God discusses the Antichrist in His Word is not to encourage us to idly speculate about him or to make us fearful. It is to warn us about him and what to watch for. The reason is that the spirit of antichrist already exists in the world, but the supreme Antichrist will appear at some future time—I believe in the *near* future.

The following mock interview is one chat I use at my meetings and conferences on the end times. I have included it in this book to illustrate and summarize all that we have learned about the Antichrist so far and to give some additional insight into his actions during that day. This simple drama is not designed to glorify the Antichrist, but to simply explain our point of view and his point of view. Every word I've written is meant to exalt Jesus and show the depravity and the terribleness of the Antichrist and his "mentor," Satan.

Imagine the interview format to be that of a lead story for a major magazine. If we, the overcoming church, would be on the earth the same time as the Antichrist's rise, it might go a little something like this.

Marilyn: *I can't honestly say that I'm delighted to have you here, but I can say that I want to ask you some questions, because I think there are many people who want to have answers about you. And I think that this interview will be helpful. So in that context I want to thank you for coming and being willing to do this.*

Male: *And I want to thank you, Mrs. Hickey, for allowing me to be here. I was ready for a nap a little earlier as you told those fairy tales of lord Satan, but I'm prepared to answer your questions now.*

Marilyn: *I'm glad you didn't take a nap and that you at least got yourself awakened enough to answer some questions. So if you're going to be a little sarcastic, I guess I'll have to be too. Who are you really?*

Male: *Well, you see, as my spirit comes into the earth, you need to understand that every spirit that does not acknowledge that Jesus came in the flesh is not of God. I'm not of God. That's what is meant by antichrist. And you've been told my spirit will come; here I am in the world already.*

Marilyn: *And you're bragging that you're not of God?*

Male: *Absolutely.*

Marilyn: *Now I want to ask you another question. Where did you really come from? What's your source?*

Male: *As those two witnesses of yours will have completed their testimony, then I, the beast, shall come forth from the bottomless pit, and I'll wage war with them, and I'll defeat them. In fact, I'm going to kill them and then throw them in the street to rot like the garbage they are.*

Marilyn: *Now, wait a minute. You're not telling the whole story. You're just telling your half. Those two witnesses....*

Male: *There is no other story.*

Marilyn: *Oh yes, those two witnesses are going to come, and it's true they will die. But remember, after three and a half days, they arise from the dead. You tell your half, and let me finish the whole thing. Now wait a minute; don't get mad at me, because I want to ask you some more questions. Who gives you your power and authority anyway as the antichrist?*

Male: *Well, my father.*

Marilyn: *Who is your father?*

Male: *Satan. Satan is my father.*

Marilyn: *You call him your father?*

Male: *Absolutely. He gives me the power and authority. As a matter of fact, through that power, people are going to be saying, "Who can stand against the beast? How great is the beast!" and they're right! How powerful I am.*

Marilyn: *But how temporary your power is. Now, don't get mad at me. Let me ask you another question. When will you appear? Everybody's watching, watching, watching, watching, and wondering when the antichrist will appear.*

Male: *Well, if you look around, my secret power is already at work in the world. As a mater of fact, that secret power is only temporary, at least until the restrainer of the church is off the scene. And what a glorious day that's going to be!*

Marilyn: *You mean when the church goes up in the Rapture.*

Male: *Yeah, let them be gone, that supposed salt of the earth. They're more like poison to me.*

Marilyn: *And so they keep you back; their presence keeps you back at this time.*

Male: *Yes, yes, yes.*

Marilyn: *I'm glad you admit it. Let me just ask a little more here, if you don't mind. You're being so gracious about answering questions—sarcastic, but gracious. Who will help you when the church is gone? You are going to be evidencing great power. Who is going to help you do that, and who's going to stand with you?*

Male: *Well, if Christians would read that book that you so dearly love.*

Marilyn: *Are you talking about the Bible?*

Male: *Yes, yes. They'd know the answer. As a matter of fact, if they read in Daniel, they would know of a beast, a dreadful and powerful beast; a beast with iron teeth and claws of bronze; a beast that will trample upon anything that's left. As a matter of fact, it'll be a beast like no other that proceeded it. It'll have ten horns, ten countries. That's my confederacy. And as Daniel was studying the ten horns, he looked and he saw a smaller horn, coming up out of those ten—actually, it uprooted the first three—but like no other horn before.*

In fact, he described it as a man with eyes, and it had a mouth that spoke such proud words. I kind of like that description of me, don't you? The problem was....

Marilyn: *Not really. I don't like it. Go ahead.*

Male: *Unfortunately, your John the Revelator actually saw through the ten horns. He was able to see that mystery and realized that it was nothing but ten kings who had yet to reign. Now these ten kings will serve only but for an hour to share their royal authority with me, the beast. As a matter of fact, their sole purpose is to confer their power and authority to me.*

Marilyn: *And you love power, don't you?*

Male: *Oh, it's delightful.*

Marilyn: *I just want to go back over this a little bit, because I want everyone who reads this to understand about those ten kingdoms, or ten nations, that are your confederacy.*

Male: *Yes.*

Marilyn: *I see that three different times in the Bible. I see it with Nebuchadnezzar when he has that dream, and he sees the head of gold, the arms of silver, stomach of brass, legs of iron, and feet of iron and clay. And it has ten toes. You know, 1 see that.*

Then I see Daniel having a dream that's very similar, only he sees the head of gold as a lion; he sees the arms as a bear; then he sees the brass stomach as a leopard. He sees that iron creature you're talking about with those ten horns. So we keep coming up with those ten kingdoms.

In Revelation, of course, John sees the ten horns again. But Daniel's the one who really tells about your coming along as that little horn sticking up and conquering three of them, and then the other seven saying, "Don't fight with us; don't fight with us! We'll just come along with you." So actually three different writers tell about that confederacy. But you don't get the whole world, do you?

Male: *Well, let's not forget, I'm exceedingly strong with the power to devour.*

Marilyn: *You're exceedingly strong with a limited time and limited power. Tell me again who gives you your power; I want to be real secure about this, and I want everybody to know it.*

Male: *My father, lord Satan.*

Marilyn: *Now from what geographical location are you going to come? I mean, if we wanted to watch today and say, "Where's the antichrist going to come from?" where will you come from?*

Male: *I'll answer by saying that if I were you, I would examine the Old Roman Empire, for out of the four prominent horns, or countries, there shall be a small horn that will rise up and show tremendous strength to the south and to the east, and to the fairest of all lands.*

Marilyn: *Is that Israel we're speaking of?*

Male: *You can figure it out for yourself.*

Marilyn: *Thanks so much. So you will come out of the Old Roman Empire, because those ten toes that Nebuchadnezzar saw in his dream are part of the old*

Roman Empire. Then those ten horns are part of the old Roman Empire. So that's what John is saying. Actually, you're going to come from some place around the Mediterranean, correct?

Male: *You've read the Word; you obviously know.*

Marilyn: *Some place in that area. I would like to define it, maybe Syria, ancient Syria. Would you be willing to say yes to that?*

Male: *I...ah....*

Marilyn: *You don't want to answer everything.*

Male: *I'd rather...not say.*

Marilyn: *I notice you have your head covered, and you have a dark hat on, so all I can really see are your eyes and your hands. But according to the Bible, you've got a wound in your head. Ah, you've got it well covered. You don't want anybody to see it, do you?*

Male: *Well, it's no big thing.*

Marilyn: *Where did you get it?*

Male: *Well, you understand that I, too, will be able to perform signs and wonders, great miracles. In fact, these will be used to actually deceive the inhabitants of the earth. As a matter of fact, they'll adore me so much that they'll create an image in my honor. And, you see, the wound is merely a counterfeit, something to take away from this death and resurrection of your Christ.*

Marilyn: *Let me get this really clear. In other words, from what I see in the Scriptures, Jesus died and rose from the dead so you have to counterfeit everything He is to be the Antichrist. So, it appears you're going to die, maybe get shot in the head. Then you will come back to life, and so people will say that it is a resurrection.*

Male: *Just to prove that I'm as powerful.*

Marilyn: *That helps me understand where the Bible says that he was, and is not, and shall be, and where it says that he is the seventh and will die and he is the eighth. Let me ask you just one more question. I'll say this, you've been patient to answer questions. Who is the false prophet that's going to help you anyway?*

Male: *As your good book says, he, too, will be a beast that will come forth from the mouth of the earth. As a matter of fact, he will wield great power.*

Marilyn: *Okay, we've got it. We've got the picture. Don't tell us anything more. That's terrible.*

THREAD OF DECEPTION

Of course, this interview is not real. It is meant to provide a summary of the Antichrist's work on earth. Let's review what's been presented here.

Before the Rapture, the prayers of the saints keep evil from completely running rampant on this earth. Christians are the salt that prevents the decay of Satan's corruption.[1] When our prayers and authority are taken from the earth, via the Rapture, the devil's power can finally blossom to its full force and take shape in the person of the Antichrist.

After the church is raptured from the earth, the Holy Spirit will remain here. Later in this book, we will observe that the Holy Spirit is present during the Tribulation because the prompting of the Holy Spirit saves many people. Thus, the powers of the devil are hindered, not by the Holy Spirit, but by the body of Christ. Jesus told us in His Word that whatsoever we bind on earth will be bound in heaven. (Matt. 16:19.) You could say that we have the authority, and the Holy Spirit does our bidding.[1] So it is the church, not the Holy Spirit, who hinders the Antichrist from being revealed, and we continue to do so until the moment we are raptured.

The thread of Satan's deceptive work can be traced throughout the Bible, from Genesis through Revelation, but his work will reach its climax in the Antichrist because this end-time personality will receive his evil power and authority from Satan himself. But we can stand as conquerors as the evil days hit by standing on the Word of God. While the world may have some hard times coming on earth, we who believe have some wonderful times ahead. Nothing that Satan can bring against us can overcome the Word of God. The Bible reveals that as believers, we are the ultimate winners!

SECTION 4

END-TIME
EVENTS

CHAPTER 10

THE CATCHING AWAY

The Master himself will give the command. Archangel
thunder! God's trumpet blast! He'll come down from
heaven and the dead in Christ will rise—they'll go first.
Then the rest of us who are still alive at the time will be
caught up with them into the clouds to meet the Master.
1 Thessalonians 4:16,17 MESSAGE

Earlier I told you that one of the major themes of Revelation and the end times is regeneration. During the
Tribulation, God will restore this world to its original pre-curse condition using fire, earthquakes, and floods. These
"birthing pains" will cause great torment to the people on
earth. Many will die; others will wish they were dead.

God does not want His children to experience these horrors. In a tender act of protection, much like a father pulling
his child from the dangers of deep water, God's Son Jesus will
gather us in His arms.

This gathering together to Christ is the Rapture. Remember there is more than one Rapture, but in this chapter we will look at the first Rapture. When that occurs Jesus will not return to earth to retrieve us; instead, the Christians who are both living and dead will meet Him in the clouds. Let's read about it from the *King James Bible* version:

> For the Lord himself shall descend from heaven with a shout, with the voice of the archangel, and with the trump of God: and the dead in Christ shall rise first:
>
> Then we which are alive and remain shall be *caught up* together with them in the clouds, to meet the Lord in the air: and so shall we ever be with the Lord.
>
> 1 Thessalonians 4:16,17

The phrase "caught up" in this verse is translated from the Greek word *harpazo*, which means "...pluck, pull, take (by force)."[1] This same idea of a physical rescue was expressed by Daniel when he prophesied, "...and there shall be a time of trouble, such as never was since there was a nation even to that same time: and at that time thy people shall be delivered, every one that shall be found written in the book" (Dan. 12:1).

Here, the Hebrew word for "delivered," is *malat*, which means to "release or rescue...speedily."[2] Daniel's prophecy has to do with the Jews in the end times. But it gives encouragement to every believer to know that God is in control and will accomplish His purposes in spite of Satan's evil forces. The Lord assured Daniel (and us) that those believers who are alive in that day will be delivered.[3]

Daniel 12:2 continues to encourage with the assurance that the ones who die will be resurrected to be with the Lord in glory:

160

And many of those who sleep in the dust of the earth shall awake, some to everlasting life....

While there are references to the Rapture in the Scriptures, the word *Rapture* does not appear in the Bible in talking about this catching away. In modern English, the word means "a state of ecstasy."[4] While this English meaning can refer to our being in an eternal state of ecstasy when we are finally with our Lord, the term is actually derived from the Latin word *rapere*, which means "to seize."[5] Thus, our being "seized" into heaven became known as the Rapture.

IN THE TWINKLING OF AN EYE

The world will neither see nor hear Christ when the Rapture occurs—they won't even know anything like that has happened. All they'll know is that a multitude of people are missing. The Word says only Christians can hear the trumpet of God and the shout of Jesus as this first seal of the title deed of the earth is opened.[6] All the world will experience is that one second we will be on earth standing side-by-side with our co-workers, friends, or loved ones, and the next second we will be gone.

> Two women shall be grinding together; the one shall be taken, and the other left.
>
> Two men shall be in the field; the one shall be taken, and the other left.
>
> Luke 17:35,36

The Rapture will happen incredibly fast—in a moment, in the twinkling of an eye according to 1 Corinthians 15:52. In this verse, the Greek word for *moment* is *atomos*, which means "uncut, i.e. (by implication) indivisible [an 'atom' of time]."[7]

When something is indivisible, it is so microscopically small that it cannot become any smaller. Imagine a measure of time that is so fast that it could not be any faster—much like the speed of light. The Rapture of the church will be even faster!

The world will not see what happens to us on that day, but they will come up with many reasons for our departure, including a mass conspiracy or abduction by UFOs. Only a few people on earth will comprehend what has really happened and turn to God as a result.

In 1 Thessalonians 4:16 we saw that during the Rapture the dead in Christ shall rise first. We can read about the Rapture in more than one place in the Bible. Here are some other Scripture references referring to the dead in Christ rising first during this divine event.

As for me, I will behold thy face in righteousness: I shall be satisfied, when I awake, with thy likeness.

Psalm 17:15

Verily, verily, I say unto you, The hour is coming, and now is, when the dead shall hear the voice of the Son of God: and they that hear shall live.

John 5:25

For as in Adam all die, even so in Christ shall all be made alive.

But every man in his own order: Christ the firstfruits; afterward they that are Christ's at his coming.

> In a moment, in the twinkling of an eye, at the last trump: for the trumpet shall sound, and the dead shall be raised incorruptible, and we shall be changed.
>
> 1 Corinthians 15:22,23,52

As soon as the dead in Christ rise up, the living will be physically caught up into the clouds to meet our Lord for the first time. Revelation 12:5 symbolically reveals this "catching away."

> And she brought forth a man child, who was to rule all nations with a rod of iron: and her child was caught up unto God, and to his throne.

The "man child" spoken of here represents the whole body of the "true saints." For we who will be "caught up unto God," it will involve the greatest change and be the most monumental, magnificent event of our lives.[8] After that occurs we will then begin our eternal fellowship and worship of Christ.

WHO WILL GO?

Anyone who does not believe in God or who has not made Christ their Lord and Savior will not go in this Rapture. We covered this in depth earlier in this book, but it is important to understand that not every person who goes to church and calls themselves a Christian will be involved in this pre-Tribulation Rapture. For one thing, we need to have a relationship with God through daily time spent in fellowship (or talking) with Him and in reading the Scriptures.

Revelation 12 pictures the Rapture as a woman travailing in childbirth. The baby boy she delivers has the authority to "rule all nations with a rod of iron" and is seen being "caught up unto God, and to his throne."[9]

We know that the woman is the entire Christian church because she is clothed with the sun and wearing a crown of twelve stars.[10] The sun shows that she is the light of the world; the twelve stars represent the twelve apostles. The moon under her feet shows that she has the powers of darkness under her. And as we just saw, the child she delivers is the overcoming church."[11]

Similarly, in Revelation 3, Christ calls the churches by name. The Laodicean church is left behind at the Rapture basically because these people do not know Christ. God has an interesting way of describing this:

> **So then because thou art lukewarm, and neither cold nor hot, I will spue thee out of my mouth.**
>
> **Revelation 3:16**

I believe that they are the backsliders and lukewarm Christians who warm the pews. They neither love nor hate Christ—they are indifferent. As Matthew Henry explains, "...They thought they were very well already, and therefore they were very indifferent whether they grew better or not...."[12] When these kind of people gather for services, they do not invite God into their midst. Yet He still tries to get their attention.

> **Behold, I stand at the door, and knock: if any man hear my voice, and open the door, I will come in to him, and will sup with him, and he with me.**
>
> **Revelation 3:20**

On the other hand, the overcoming Christians are the Philadelphian church type of believers mentioned in this chapter. They are the ones who keep God's Word and stand on it in patience and faith. Christ promised them that He would keep them "...from the hour of temptation [the Tribulation], which shall come upon all the world..." (Rev. 3:10). That promise is for us too—He will deliver us from the wrath of the Tribulation that is to come.

SAFE FROM THE ENEMY'S ATTACK

Satan will try to keep the church from entering into heaven, engaging in a battle with the archangel, Michael. The dragon won't be able to keep the saints from gathering with Christ, and his bitter contest will end with his expulsion from the heavens[13] and the end of his reign as prince of the power of the air.[14]

In anger, Satan will set out to destroy the remnant church—the lukewarm Christians who turn to God after the Rapture.

> Therefore rejoice, ye heavens, and ye that dwell in them. Woe to the inhabiters of the earth and of the sea! for the devil is come down unto you, having great wrath, because he knoweth that he hath but a short time.
>
> And when the dragon saw that he was cast unto the earth, he persecuted the woman which brought forth the man child.
>
> And to the woman were given two wings of a great eagle, that she might fly into the wilderness, into her place, where she is nourished for a time, and times, and half a time, from the face of the serpent.

And the serpent cast out of his mouth water as a flood after the woman, that he might cause her to be carried away of the flood.

And the earth helped the woman, and the earth opened her mouth, and swallowed up the flood which the dragon cast out of his mouth.

And the dragon was wroth with the woman, and went to make war with the remnant of her seed, which keep the commandments of God, and have the testimony of Jesus Christ.

Revelation 12:12-17

Verse 16 suggests that nature will somehow protect these new Christians. Perhaps they will flee to the mountains. Or some kind of divine intervention could happen; they could be helped in some unexpected way. Flooding or overflowing water is often seen in Scriptures as a type of strong enemy as in Psalm 18:16 that says, "He sent from above, he took me, he drew me out of many waters."

Whatever the source of help, in John's end-time vision, he saw that the remnant church will be safe from the enemy's attack and that to preserve and protect it, something will take place as wonderful as if the earth would suddenly open and swallow up a powerful flood.[15]

CHAPTER 11

SEVEN YEARS OF TROUBLE, PART 1

The Tribulation begins after the Rapture. Its source is found in the conflict between God and Satan, described in Genesis 3:15, but it does not just happen. It is triggered by the Antichrist's rise out of the revived Roman Empire. Ironically, his push for peace with the nations of the world marks the beginning of this seven-year period of trouble, anguish, and eventual war.

The actual term *tribulation* is used only a handful of times in the Bible in referring to this final episode of world history (as we know it), but it is described in many Scriptures (Exodus 15, Matthew 24, and Mark 13, to name a few). Other terms the Bible uses to depict it are punishment (Isa. 24:20-23), trouble (Jer. 30:7), destruction (Joel 1:15), and darkness (Joel 2:2).

The original Greek word for *tribulation* is *thlipsis*, which means "afflicted (-tion), anguish, burdened, persecution, tribulation, trouble."[1] One dictionary defines *tribulation* as "distress or suffering resulting from oppression or persecution; *also*: a trying experience."[2]

The entire Tribulation period will be seven years long and is broken down into two time periods of three and a half years. The first three and one-half years will be marked by a false sense of peace (although it will still be a time of trouble) as the master deceiver causes the world to believe that he has achieved world peace among the nations. The second half, or the Great Tribulation, will definitely be "a trying experience." We have seen that certain events will cause the Antichrist to break this covenant of peace. This will lead to the second three and a half years of colossal scenes of trouble and turmoil in a magnitude never before experienced on earth.

Many people have wondered how we know that the Tribulation only lasts for seven years. The secret is revealed in a numbering pattern representing time. This pattern is found in the book of Daniel and is often referred to as Daniel's Seventy Weeks. In fact, the prophet Daniel called the period of the Tribulation the final week in his Seventy Weeks vision.

DANIEL'S SEVENTY WEEKS

Seventy weeks are determined upon thy people and upon thy holy city, to finish the transgression, and to make an end of sins, and to make reconciliation for iniquity, and to bring in everlasting righteousness, and to seal up the vision and prophecy, and to anoint the most Holy.

Know therefore and understand, that from the going forth of the commandment to restore and to build Jerusalem unto the Messiah the Prince shall be seven weeks, and threescore and two weeks: the street shall be built again, and the wall, even in troublous times.

And after threescore and two weeks shall Messiah be cut off, but not for himself: and the people of the prince that shall come shall destroy the city and the sanctuary; and the end thereof shall be with a flood, and unto the end of the war desolations are determined.

And he shall confirm the covenant with many for one week: and in the midst of the week he shall cause the sacrifice and the oblation to cease, and for the overspreading of abominations he shall make it desolate, even until the consummation, and that determined shall be poured upon the desolate.

Daniel 9:24-27

In this passage Daniel said that seventy "weeks," or years, would elapse between the Israelites' return to Jerusalem to rebuild the city and temple and the advent of the Messiah to rule this world. One week (7 days) counts for seven years (1 day of the week = 1year) in this prophecy. Therefore, 70 weeks would multiply by 7 to yield a total of 490 years. This time period is called the Jewish Age and lasts for 490 years (70 times 7).

Jesus arrived 483 years after the temple's rebuilding. When the Jews rejected Him, the Jewish Age was suspended and the Church Age began. The Jewish Age will resume again when the church is raptured, but only one week remains on the clock. This means the time between the Rapture of the church and the advent of the Messiah as Prince of this world is only seven years (483 plus 7 = 490).

Daniel described this final week in Daniel 9:27 as a time when the sacrifices and feasts will cease and the Antichrist will erect his idol, the "abomination of desolation," in the temple.

This passage indicates that at the end of the Tribulation, which is the end of the Jewish Age, the Lord will return from heaven with His saints and angels to make an end of sins, to make reconciliation for iniquity, to bring in everlasting righteousness, to seal up the vision and prophecy, "and to anoint the most Holy."[3]

This "reconciliation for iniquity" is what Jesus was referring to in Matthew 13:40 when He said, "As therefore the tares are gathered and burned in the fire; so shall it be in the end of this world." The word *world* in this verse does not mean "world" in English. It is the Greek word *aion*, which means "age," as in a period of time.[4] From these Scriptures we can see that at the end of the Jewish Age will come the judgment of the sinners (tares).

THE ANTICHRIST

We have already covered the Antichrist—his names, the area where he may come from, what army he'll head, the countries he'll rule, his role in the last days, the havoc he'll wreak. But remember that all this takes place during the Tribulation period. That's when Satan's power will finally be unleashed in full force and take shape in the person of this major end-time figure, because just prior to that time our prayers and authority will be taken from the earth due to the Rapture.

ANGELIC SERMONS

Humankind will be so preoccupied with its pain caused by the Antichrist's rule during this time that what little energy people have will be conserved for the mere act of surviving.

The Gospel message will be preached, however, in a unique move of God—the preaching will come from an angel who declares the Gospel from heaven to people on earth. This angel will prophesy the fall of the Antichrist's kingdom and religion, telling people not to take the mark of the beast.

> And I saw another angel fly in the midst of heaven, having the everlasting gospel to preach unto them that dwell on the earth, and to every nation, and kindred, and tongue, and people,
>
> Saying with a loud voice, Fear God, and give glory to him; for the hour of his judgment is come: and worship him that made heaven, and earth, and the sea, and the fountains of waters.
>
> And there followed another angel, saying, Babylon is fallen, is fallen, that great city, because she made all nations drink of the wine of the wrath of her fornication.
>
> And the third angel followed them, saying with a loud voice, If any man worship the beast and his image, and receive his mark in his forehead, or in his hand,
>
> The same shall drink of the wine of the wrath of God, which is poured out without mixture into the cup of his indignation; and he shall be tormented with fire and brimstone in the pres ence of the holy angels, and in the presence of the Lamb:
>
> And the smoke of their torment ascendeth up for ever and ever: and they have no rest day nor night, who worship the beast and his image, and whosoever receiveth the mark of his name.

> Here is the patience of the saints: here are they that keep the commandments of God, and the faith of Jesus.
>
> And I heard a voice from heaven saying unto me, Write, Blessed are the dead which die in the Lord from henceforth: Yea, saith the Spirit, that they may rest from their labours; and their works do follow them.
>
> Revelation 14:6-13

Some people believe the Holy Spirit will be removed from the earth at the Rapture. That theory does not follow the Bible's words, because it is through the Holy Spirit's drawing that we come to know Christ.[5] Without the Holy Spirit's drawing power, people could not be saved during the Tribulation.

In fact, the Holy Spirit will move in incredible ways because the greatest time of evangelism on this earth will be during the Tribulation period.

END-TIME REVIVAL

Masses of people will turn to the Lord. The masses will be so great that they will populate the earth during the beginning of the Millennium.

The Bible doesn't give a number of how many people will be saved during this early part of the Tribulation, but Revelation 7:9 says that the amount of people saved will be more than a man could count.

> After this I beheld, and, lo, a great multitude, which no man could number, of all nations, and kindreds, and people, and tongues, stood before the throne, and before the Lamb, clothed with white robes, and palms in their hands.
>
> Revelation 7:9

Notice the Scripture says that these Tribulation saints are of "all nations, and kindreds, and people, and tongues." That means that this revival will spread throughout the entire world during the Tribulation.

In this book we have seen the first few seals opened and what they represent. When Christ opens the fifth seal of the title deed to the earth, we see those Tribulation saints raptured into heaven, standing before the Lamb, dressed in garments washed white as snow and holding palm leaves.[6]

These palm leaves the saints carry in Revelation 7:9 are very important because they represent victory. In the Bible, the Israelites used palm leaves to remind them of the victories God gave them over their enemies in battles and storms. These Tribulation saints standing before Jesus will wave their palms to honor the victory God gives over death and hell.

HIDING IN CAVES

The final event before the end of the first three and a half years of the Tribulation is the opening of the sixth seal. Up to this point, heaven had orchestrated the Antichrist's rise to power and mankind's positioning to make a decision between God or Satan. With the sixth seal comes the beginning of God's powerful forces moving violently on the earth.

> And I beheld when he had opened the sixth seal, and, lo, there was a great earthquake; and the sun became black as sackcloth of hair, and the moon became as blood;
>
> And the stars of heaven fell unto the earth, even as a fig tree casteth her untimely figs, when she is shaken of a mighty wind.

And the heaven departed as a scroll when it is rolled together; and every mountain and island were moved out of their places.

And the kings of the earth, and the great men, and the rich men, and the chief captains, and the mighty men, and every bondman, and every free man, hid themselves in the dens and in the rocks of the mountains;

And said to the mountains and rocks, Fall on us, and hide us from the face of him that sitteth on the throne, and from the wrath of the Lamb:

For the great day of his wrath is come; and who shall be able to stand?

Revelation 6:12-17

This sixth seal will bring great natural catastrophes:

- the incredible earthquakes
- the sun becomes black
- the moon turns red
- the stars fall
- the wind ravages trees and fields
- the mountains and islands are moved out of place

People will hide in caves and ask the rocks to kill them so they can be saved from God's wrath.[7]

As the devastation of the sixth seal indicates, the second half of the Tribulation will be much worse. It will be an intense time of distress and suffering. In fact, God calls it the "Great Tribulation," meaning the horrors will increase for man and the devil.[8] And it is very similar to the last three and one-half years of Daniel's final week in his Seventy Weeks prophecy.

THE SECOND HALF

Just before the seventh seal is opened, everything will fall silent in heaven for a half-hour while God prepares and delivers His people before the devastating judgments of the final seal are unleashed on the earth. The whole earth will stand in awe.

And when he had opened the seventh seal, there was silence in heaven about the space of half an hour.

Revelation 8:1

This last three and a half years of the Tribulation, called the "Great Tribulation," will be filled with much pain, death, and destruction for people, animals, earth, and the heavens. Before this begins, however, God will perform a great act of love for His people.

First, the angel holding God's seal will instruct the four angels in charge of the north, south, east, and west winds to halt their destruction. Before these angels carry out the judgments on the earth, God's loving mercy will seal 144,000 people.

Hurt not the earth, neither the sea, nor the trees, till we have sealed the servants of our God in their foreheads. And I heard the number of them which were sealed: *and there were* sealed an hundred *and* forty *and* four thousand of all the tribes of the *children of Israel.*

Revelation 7:3,4

We have seen that these 144,000 people are Jews, 12,000 from each of the twelve tribes of Israel.[9] God will write His name on their foreheads with a mark.

> And I looked, and, lo, a Lamb stood on the mount Sion, and with him an hundred forty *and* four thousand, having his Father's name written in their foreheads.
>
> Revelation 14:1

I believe this mark will be as real and visible as the mark of the beast in Revelation 13:16-17.

Secondly, God will resurrect the dead in Christ and rapture the Tribulation saints who are still alive. This is sometimes referred to as the Great Harvest Rapture. During this activity, God will separate the wheat from the tares as we saw Jesus talk about in Matthew 13. An act of God's mercy, this Rapture will rescue the Gentiles who accepted Christ during the first three and a half years of great torture, despair, and trouble.

> After this I beheld, and, lo, a great multitude, which no man could number, of all nations, and kindreds, and people, and tongues, stood before the throne, and before the Lamb, clothed with white robes, and palms in their hands;
>
> And cried with a loud voice, saying, Salvation to our God which sitteth upon the throne, and unto the Lamb.
>
> And all the angels stood round about the throne, and about the elders and the four beasts, and fell before the throne on their faces, and worshipped God,
>
> Saying, Amen: Blessing, and glory, and wisdom, and thanks giving, and honour, and power, and might, be unto our God for ever and ever. Amen.
>
> And one of the elders answered, saying unto me, What are these which are arrayed in white robes? and whence came they?

And I said unto him, Sir, thou knowest. And he said to me, These are they which came out of great tribulation, and have washed their robes, and made them white in the blood of the Lamb.

Therefore are they before the throne of God, and serve him day and night in his temple: and he that sitteth on the throne shall dwell among them.

They shall hunger no more, neither thirst any more; neither shall the sun light on them, nor any heat.

For the Lamb which is in the midst of the throne shall feed them, and shall lead them unto living fountains of waters: and God shall wipe away all tears from their eyes.

Revelation 7:9-17

What is the difference between these two groups (the Gentiles who accept Christ during this time and the 144,000)? Why would God leave one group of His people on earth while He takes the other group into heaven?

GOSPEL MESSENGERS

God does this because His full attention is now being turned to the Jews. He will send them as messengers of the Gospel. These 144,000 Jews will be protected from the coming plagues and the wrath of the Antichrist so they can witness to the world and to Israel.[10]

The 144,000 are the first fruits of the Jews, people who are spiritual "virgins," having never dabbled in a religion that was not from God nor worshiped or followed the beast. Revelation 14:4 describes them as being "...not defiled with women;

177

for they are virgins...[they] follow the Lamb whithersoever he goeth... [and] were redeemed from among men, being the firstfruits unto God and to the Lamb."

The Bible often uses adultery and fornication as a picture for spiritual unfaithfulness. Because the 144,000 stayed true to God and waited for Him to fulfill their desires in life, they are referred to as "virgins" in this verse.

"Virgin" can also be taken literally to mean that these people had not been defiled by sexual indiscretions. The reason this may be taken literally is that Jesus said, "As the days of Noe were, so shall also the coming of the Son of man be" (Matt. 24:37). He explained that people will eat and drink, marry, and give in marriage, fulfilling their every desire without respect for self, others, or God—just as people did before the flood in Noah's time.

This carnality will be rampant during the Tribulation. Sex and every form of physical indulgence will have free reign.[11] However, God always has a remnant. He will set these 144,000 people apart because (1) they are Jewish; (2) they have remained true to God; (3) they have accepted Christ; and (4) they are physically pure.

Eventually, we see them on Mt. Sion singing "a new song" before Jesus and with the other saints in heaven, a song that no one else on earth can learn.

> And I looked, and, lo, a Lamb stood on the *mount Sion, and with him an hundred forty and four thousand,* having his Father's name written in their foreheads.

And I heard a voice from heaven, as the voice of many waters, and as the voice of a great thunder: and I heard the voice of harpers harping with their harps:

And they sung as it were a new song before the throne, and before the four beasts, and the elders: and no man could learn that song but the hundred and forty and four thousand, which were redeemed from the earth.

These are they which were not defiled with women; for they are virgins. These are they which follow the Lamb whithersoever he goeth. These were redeemed from among men, being the firstfruits unto God and to the Lamb.

And in their mouth was found no guile: for they are without fault before the throne of God

Revelation 14:1-5

Harps will play in heaven, and all in heaven will join in this service of incredible worship. The 144,000 will have a special relationship with the Lamb because they will recognize that He is their Messiah, Savior, and Redeemer.

THE TRIBULATION SAINTS

The Tribulation saints will be part of the worship service of the 144,000, but this event will take place after they have already held a private service in heaven following their Rapture. They will stand before the Lord dressed in robes that have been washed white by the blood of the Lamb, playing harps and singing a very important song:

And *they sing the song of Moses* the servant of God, and the song of the Lamb, saying, Great and marvellous are

thy works, Lord God Almighty; just and true are thy
ways, thou King of saints.

Revelation 15:3

This isn't the "new song" of the 144,000; in fact, it is a very
ancient song. Moses wrote it after God parted the Red Sea,
allowing the Israelites to pass into safety, and then brought
the waters back together, destroying Pharaoh and his army.
Notice how Moses' song of victory tells the story of the Tribulation saints:

> Then sang Moses and the children of Israel this song unto
> the Lord, and spake, saying, I will sing unto the Lord, for
> he hath triumphed gloriously: the horse and his rider
> hath he thrown into the sea.
>
> The Lord is my strength and song, and he is become my
> salvation: he is my God, and I will prepare him an habita-
> tion; my father's God, and I will exalt him.
>
> The Lord is a man of war: the Lord is his name.
>
> Thy right hand, O Lord, is become glorious in power: thy
> right hand, O Lord, hath dashed in pieces the enemy.
>
> And in the greatness of thine excellency thou hast over-
> thrown them that rose up against thee: thou sentest forth
> thy wrath, which consumed them as stubble.
>
> The enemy said, I will pursue, I will overtake, I will divide
> the spoil; my lust shall be satisfied upon them; I will draw
> my sword, my hand shall destroy them.
>
> Who is like unto thee, O Lord, among the gods? who is like
> thee, glorious in holiness, fearful in praises, doing wonders?

Thou in thy mercy hast led forth the people which thou
hast redeemed: thou hast guided them in thy strength
unto thy holy habitation

Thou shalt bring them in, and plant them in the mountain of thine inheritance, in the place, O Lord, which thou
hast made for thee to dwell in, in the Sanctuary, O Lord,
which thy hands have established.

The Lord shall reign for ever and ever.

Exodus 15:1-3,6,7,9,11,13,17,18

The Israelites still had many trials and battles to face
before they could enter and claim the Promised Land, but
their song praised God for fulfilling all His promises in their
lives. Similarly, the Tribulation saints in heaven will rejoice
because of their victory over the Antichrist through God's
unusual deliverance. These saints will praise the Lord for His
complete work giving His chosen their full inheritance.

PICTURE OF THE END TIMES

The story of the Exodus, God's delivery of the Israelites out
of bondage and into a land of promise, is a beautiful picture
of the end times. In Exodus, Pharaoh represents a foreshadowing of the Antichrist, and the plagues provide a glimpse of
what the trumpet/vial judgments in the book of Revelation
will be like.

With the plagues in Exodus, God utilized nature to speak
to man. These plagues of nature showed man where he was
deceived. They served as judgment for man and showed the
Egyptians that their gods were false and powerless.[12] Because

they worshiped such things as the Nile, frogs, locusts, and their firstborn children, God used those very things against the Egyptians to discredit their gods.

As the *International Standard Bible Encyclopaedia* explains, "...The magicians who claimed to represent the gods of Egypt were defeated, Pharaoh himself, who was accounted divine, was humbled, the great god, the Nile, was polluted, frogs defiled the temples and, at last, the sun, the greatest god of Egypt, was blotted out in darkness."[13]

If you are familiar with this story, you'll remember that those who paid attention to the message of God's plagues found deliverance out of Egypt. Those who placed the mark of God (the blood of a slain lamb) on their doors were spared death in their families during the final plague.

> **And thus shall ye eat it; with your loins girded, your shoes on your feet, and your staff in your hand; and ye shall eat it in haste: it is the Lord's passover.**
>
> **For I will pass through the land of Egypt this night, and will smite all the firstborn in the land of Egypt, both man and beast; and against all the gods of Egypt I will execute judgment: I am the Lord.**
>
> **And the blood shall be to you for a token upon the houses where ye are: and when I see the blood, I will pass over you, and the plague shall not be upon you to destroy you, when I smite the land of Egypt.**
>
> **Exodus 12:11-13**

Although it was mainly God's chosen people, the Israelites, who understood the lessons of the plagues and followed

God's commandments, a few Egyptians understood and left during the Exodus.[14]

The same will happen during the Tribulation. The people who understand the message of the seven trumpet/vial judgments (which we'll look at in the next chapter) will realize that the devil's power counts for nothing when compared with God's.

Each plague that falls on man and the earth will prove that Satan ultimately has no control over the world and is unworthy of their worship.

Remember, people who have listened to the messages from heaven and to the many signs that have come from the previous six seals will be delivered from the earth in the mid Tribulation Rapture.

THE TWO WITNESSES

And I will give power unto my two witnesses, and they shall prophesy a thousand two hundred and threescore days, clothed in sackcloth.

Revelation 11:3

Soon after God "catches away" the Tribulation saints and seals the 144,000, He will exemplify His everlasting love for people again. This time, He will bring two men into Israel to preach His Word and empower them to prophesy. These men are known as the two witnesses.

I believe that these two witnesses will be Moses and Elijah because they were on the Mount of Transfiguration with Jesus.[15] Their miracles were identical to the ones the two witnesses will perform—they will cause fire to rain down, turn water into blood, and bring other plagues.[16]

Their purpose in the Tribulation will be to harass the Antichrist and call the Jews to worship Jesus. They will remain in Israel for 1,260 days, or almost three and a half years.[17]

Zechariah prophesied of these two men in his vision of a gold candlestick and two olive trees.

> And the angel that talked with me came again....
>
> And said unto me, What seest thou? And I said, I have looked, and behold a *candlestick all of gold,* with a bowl upon the top of it, and his *seven lamps* thereon, and seven pipes to the seven lamps, which are upon the top thereof:
>
> And two olive trees by it, one upon the right side of the bowl, and the other upon the left side thereof.
>
> Zechariah 4:1-3

He saw the two witnesses as olive trees. The olive tree is a symbol of the Jews' spiritual heritage.

> Then said he, These are the two anointed ones, that stand by the Lord of the whole earth.
>
> Zechariah 4:14

In the Bible, oil is often symbolic of the anointing. In this next verse, we see that the two witnesses pour their oil, or their anointing, into the candlestick, which is the symbol for the church in Revelation.

> And I answered again, and said unto him, What be these two olive branches which through the two golden pipes empty the golden oil out of themselves?
>
> Zechariah 4:12

In his well-known commentary, Matthew Henry gave a vivid description of what the oil represented, saying, "God gave them the oil of holy zeal, and courage, and strength, and comfort; he made them olive-trees, and their lamps of profession were kept burning by the oil of inward gracious principles, which they received from God. They had oil not only in their lamps, but in their vessels—habits of spiritual life, light, and zeal."[18]

As the two witnesses zealously preach the Word during the Tribulation, their anointing will bring more and more people into Christ's church.

In the next chapter, we will see what happens to the two witnesses and look at the seven trumpet/vial judgments, which give us a bird's-eye view of heaven's judgments on mankind and the devil. As we continue to unveil the end-time mysteries and get the whole picture, it's so evident that God is in complete control of the last days and the Tribulation period.

CHAPTER 12

SEVEN YEARS OF TROUBLE, PART 2

Once God's people are protected, the seventh seal on the title deed of the earth will be opened. Out of this seal will come seven judgments—four upon the earth and three upon mankind.

Viewing these seven judgments from heaven, we see them as trumpets blown by angels. But from earth's perspective, the trumpets look like vials. Compare Revelation, Chapters 6-11, with Revelation, Chapters 12-16, and you will see that these chapters tell the same story—the first version is seen from heaven, and the second from earth (see Figure 4.1).

For instance, according to the version seen from heaven, when the second trumpet sounds, "...a great mountain burning with fire was cast into the sea: and the third part of the sea became blood; And the third part of the creatures which were in the sea, and had life, died; and the third part of the ships were destroyed" (Rev. 8:8,9). Likewise, in the version of this event seen from earth, the second vial is poured out upon the earth and affects the sea, making it "as the blood of a dead man: and every living soul died in the sea" (Rev.16:3).

The trumpet judgment shows only a third of the sea dying, but the vial judgment shows all in the sea dying. Why would the same event have two different outcomes? The difference is that the event is seen from two different perspectives. From heaven's vantage point, we can see the whole earth and that not everything is affected. But when we stand on earth, our view is limited, and it appears that the whole earth is affected.

The seven trumpet/vial judgments are discussed several times in the Bible. God describes them in Acts 2:19-20, saying, "And I will shew wonders in heaven above, and signs in the earth beneath; blood, and fire, and vapour of smoke: The sun shall be turned into darkness, and the moon into blood, before that great and notable day of the Lord come." In Haggai 2:6-7 He said, "...Yet once, it is a little while, and I will shake the heavens, and the earth, and the sea, and the dry land; And I will shake all nations...." These words echo Christ's prophecy of the Great Tribulation in Matthew.

> **Immediately after the tribulation of chose days shall the sun be darkened, and the moon shall not give her light, and the stars shall fall from heaven, and the powers of the heavens shall be shaken:**
>
> Matthew 24:29

When Jesus opens the seventh seal, these much-prophesied wonders will begin with the sounding of the trumpets in heaven. Let's look at the first one, the fiery hail.

FIRST TRUMPET—HAIL ON FIRE

The first trumpet/vial will send hail mixed with fire and blood to the earth. It will fall in the same way fire and brimstone fell on Sodom and Gomorrah in Genesis.

> Then the Lord rained upon Sodom and upon Gomorrah brimstone and fire from the Lord out of heaven;
>
> Genesis 19:24

> The first angel sounded, and there followed hail and fire mingled with blood, and they were cast upon the earth: and the third part of trees was burnt up, and all green grass was burnt up.
>
> Revelation 8:7

This fire will have a serious effect on the people who have taken the mark of the beast.

> And the first went, and poured out his vial upon the earth; and there fell a noisome and grievous sore upon the men which had the mark of the beast, and *upon* them which worshipped his image.
>
> Revelation 16:2

The Greek word for *noisome—kakos—*means "bad, evil"[1] and is used in this verse to pinpoint the plague referred to here as being terribly painful and dangerous. The Greek word for grievous—poneros—means "causing pain and trouble, bad."[2] It is added to emphasize the blistering gravity of the sores and to distinguish this plague as being exceptionally severe.

SECOND TRUMPET—OCEAN LIFE DIES

The second trumpet/vial will affect the water of the seas, turning it to blood much the same as when the Nile was judged in Exodus 7:20. As a result, most of the sea life (including seafood) will die within the ocean. People will no longer be able to rely on this natural resource for food. We have already seen Revelation 8:8 and 16:3 that refer to this. Notice their similarity to Exodus 7:20:

> **And Moses and Aaron did so, as the Lord commanded; and he lifted up the rod, and smote the waters that were in the river, in the sight of Pharaoh, and in the sight of his servants; and all the waters that were in the river were turned to blood.**

The waters became so corrupt that not only did the fish die, but there was a terribly offensive odor. Can you imagine this happening in the Tribulation? These first two prophecies alone should propel you to get right with God now if you feel that you aren't. Yet there are more detestable plagues to come.

THIRD TRUMPET—DRINKING WATER SPOILED

The third trumpet/vial will also affect the water, but this time the fire will fall on fresh water, poisoning the drinking water with wormwood.

Basically, wormwood is a plant that yields a bitter dark green oil and is actually defined as "something bitter...."[3] It is often associated with gall, which is also connected to bitterness in relation to the idea of poison.[4] This will be a huge devastation since most of the world's water supply will become contaminated and have deadly consequences for those who drink it.

> And the third angel sounded, and there fell a great star from heaven, burning as it were a lamp, and it fell upon the third part of the rivers, and upon the fountains of waters;
>
> And the name of the star is called Wormwood: and the third part of the waters became wormwood; and many men died of the waters, because they were made bitter.
>
> Revelation 8:10,11

Revelation 16 reveals that this contamination will turn the water into blood.

> And the third angel poured out his vial upon the rivers and fountains of waters; and they became blood.
>
> And I heard the angel of the waters say, Thou art righteous, O Lord, which art, and wast, and shalt be, because thou hast judged thus.
>
> For they have shed the blood of saints and prophets, and thou hast given them blood to drink; for they are worthy.
>
> And I heard another out of the altar say, Even so, Lord God Almighty, true and righteous are thy judgments.
>
> Revelation 16:4-7

This is similar to the punishment God promised the followers of Baal (a false god worshiped by the inhabitants of Canaan)[5] in Jeremiah 9:15, when He said, "...I will feed them... with wormwood, and give them water of gall to drink."

FOURTH TRUMPET—EXTREME DARKNESS AND HEAT

The fourth trumpet/vial will cause a third part of the sun, moon, and stars to darken.

> And the fourth angel sounded, and the third part of the sun was smitten, and the third part of the moon, and the third part of the stars; so as the third part of them was darkened, and the day shone not for a third part of it, and the night likewise.
>
> Revelation 8:12

The change in the sun's light will somehow increase its heat and scorch men with an intense burning.

> And the fourth angel poured out his vial upon the sun; and power was given unto him to scorch men with fire.
>
> And men were scorched with great heat, and blasphemed the name of God, which hath power over these plagues: and they repented not to give him glory.
>
> Revelation 16:8,9

God similarly judged the sun in Egypt when he caused darkness to fall over the land. The darkness was so profound that the Bible says it could even be felt:

> And the Lord said unto Moses, Stretch out thine hand toward heaven, that there may be darkness over the land of Egypt, even darkness which may be felt.
>
> And Moses stretched forth his hand toward heaven; and there was a thick darkness in all the land of Egypt three days.
>
> Exodus 10:21,22

Can you believe what we've seen so far? These first four trumpets/vials have brought great judgments upon the earth, water, and sky. We've seen a world on fire, thirsty, and scorched. Even though man will be terribly tortured by these events, these judgments were meant mainly for nature in order to cleanse the earth of the curse. But it's not over yet.

The next three trumpet/vials will be directed toward mankind exclusively. The pain and torment will be so great with these plagues that just before they begin an angel in heaven will warn those left on earth, crying out, "...Woe, woe, woe, to the inhabiters of the earth..." (Rev. 8:13).

FIFTH TRUMPET—"LOCUSTS" FROM HELL

When the fifth trumpet sounds, an angel from heaven who has been given the enormous responsibility of keeping the key to the bottomless pit will open the pit and loose "locusts" upon the earth. These "locusts" are actually demons who will have the power to torment men like scorpions. They will have bodies like horses, heads like men, hair like women, crowns of gold, teeth like lions, breastplates of iron, wings that sound like chariots running to battle, and tails with scorpion stings. They can't hurt vegetation or the 144,000 Jews; and they aren't allowed to kill men, only torture them to the point where they beg to die.

> **And the fifth angel sounded, and I saw a star fall from heaven unto the earth: and to him was given the key of the bottomless pit.**

And he opened the bottomless pit; and there arose a smoke out of the pit, as the smoke of a great furnace; and the sun and the air were darkened by reason of the smoke of the pit.

And there came out of the smoke locusts upon the earth: and unto them was given power, as the scorpions of the earth have power.

And it was commanded them that they should not hurt the grass of the earth, neither any green thing, neither any tree; but only those men which have not the seal of God in their foreheads.

And to them it was given that they should not kill them, but that they should be tormented five months: and their torment was as the torment of a scorpion, when he striketh a man.

And in those days shall men seek death, and shall not find it; and shall desire to die, and death shall flee from them.

And the shapes of the locusts were like unto horses prepared unto battle; and on their heads were as it were crowns like gold, and their faces were as the faces of men.

And they had hair as the hair of women, and their teeth were as the teeth of lions.

And they had breastplates, as it were breastplates of iron; and the sound of their wings was as the sound of chariots of many horses running to battle.

And they had tails like unto scorpions, and there were stings in their tails: and their power was to hurt men five months.

> And they had a king over them, which is the angel of the
> bottomless pit, whose name in the Hebrew tongue is Abad-
> don, but in the Greek tongue hath his name Apollyon.
>
> Revelation 9:1-11

We see here that the leader of the demon locust is Apollyon, or the destroyer, whose name is Satan.[6] For five months,
people covered with the sores produced by these demon
locusts will be forced to live in the darkness caused by the
smoke from hell covering the sun and moon.

> And the fifth angel poured out his vial upon the seat of
> the beast; and his kingdom was full of darkness; and they
> gnawed their tongues for pain,
>
> And blasphemed the God of heaven because of their pains
> and their sores, and repented not of their deeds.
>
> Revelation 16:10,11

People will speak contemptuously of God because of their
pain during this horrible time, but incredibly they will not
repent.

UNSTOPPABLE PLAGUES

As the plagues plunge the world into chaos, the Antichrist's
followers will begin to doubt him. Remember, the Jews will
turn against him at the end of the first three and a half years
of his reign, and the nations of the world will then begin to
question him. His marvelous miracles cannot quench the
fires, his tricks cannot cleanse the waters, and his charm cannot take the pain away.

At this point, his grip on the world is loosening. Two of his confederate nations will turn against him—the king of the south, probably Egypt, will war against him, and the king of the north, probably Turkey, will fiercely "come against him," bent on destroying him.

> And at the time of the end shall the king of the south push at him: and the king of the north shall come against him like a whirlwind, with chariots, and with horsemen, and with many ships; and he shall enter into the countries, and shall overflow and pass over.
>
> Daniel 11:40

The Antichrist will fight against them and win, but his fury will grow because of their uprisings.

He will aim his fury at Israel, and when the sixth angel sounds his trumpet, the Antichrist will take advantage of the situation to begin the march to Armageddon.

SIXTH TRUMPET—A THIRD OF HUMANITY KILLED

With the sixth trumpet/vial, the Euphrates River (in modern day Iraq) will dry up, freeing four fallen angels who had been bound in the river. These angels will be commanders of 200 million demon horsemen who have breastplates of fire and brimstone. The heads of their horses will be like the heads of lions, out of which come fire, smoke, and brimstone.

The horsemen will spend thirteen months on earth, killing one-third of the earth's already dwindling population with the fire, smoke, and brimstone from their own mouths.

They also will torture people with their horses' tails. Revelation 9:19 TLB describes those tails as being similar to serpents' heads, which strike and bite with fatal wounds.

The mayhem caused by the seals and the trumpet/vial judgments will greatly please the devil. He will think the demons God has set free increase his power against God. And with the Euphrates River dried up, a pathway will be opened for the kings of the east to ride into Israel for the final battle. Thus, Satan will act on the opportunities opening to him and send out three unclean spirits to gather the kings of the world together for war against God.[7]

THE VALLEY OF MEGIDDO

The world's final battle, the Battle of Armageddon, will begin in the valley of Megiddo; but it will not be fought here. Megiddo is only the gathering place.

Megiddo will be discussed in-depth later on, but basically once assembled there, the Antichrist's demon-powered army will march in absolute precision down the Valley of Jezreel toward the Jordan River valley, then head south. They will turn west near Jericho and head to Jerusalem, where the final battle will take place. Many Bible scholars believe that this is the Valley of Jehoshaphat.

JESUS CLAIMS THE EARTH

While the Antichrist is luring the world's armies to Armageddon for the final showdown, the scene in heaven will be triumphant. In Revelation 10, Jesus plants one foot on the earth and the other on the sea.

And I saw another mighty angel come down from heaven, clothed with a cloud: and a rainbow was upon his head, and his face was as it were the sun, and his feet as pillars of fire:

And he had in his hand a little book open: and he set his right foot upon the sea, and his left foot on the earth.

Revelation 10:1,2

I believe that this will not be His physical return to the earth. It will be a figurative, symbolic move that will be very significant. He will make this distinct, deliberate act in order to show that He has command of each and that His power is universal, all things being under His feet.[8] It expresses the purpose that He is going to take possession of the whole world[9] and restore it to its rightful owners—mankind.

SEVENTH TRUMPET— LAW OF INHERITANCE FULFILLED

And the seventh angel sounded; and there were great voices in heaven, saying, The kingdoms of this world are become the kingdoms of our Lord, and of his Christ; and he shall reign for ever and ever.

And the four and twenty elders, which sat before God on their seats, fell upon their faces, and worshipped God,

Saying, We give thee thanks, O Lord God Almighty, which art, and wast, and art to come; because thou hast taken to thee thy great power, and hast reigned.

And the nations were angry, and thy wrath is come, and the time of the dead, that they should be judged, and that thou shouldest give reward unto thy servants the prophets, and to the saints, and them that fear thy name, small and great; and shouldest destroy them which destroy the earth.

And the temple of God was opened in heaven, and there was seen in his temple the ark of his testament: and there were lightnings, and voices, and thunderings, and an earthquake, and great hail.

Revelation 11:15-19

With the opening of the seventh and final seal, Jesus will fulfill the law of inheritance, proving He is the rightful Heir to the world. By setting His foot upon the earth, He will legally claim the right to kick the trespasser, the devil, off His property.

The earth is the Lord's, and the fulness thereof; the world, and they that dwell therein.

Psalm 24:1

In another figurative move, Jesus will give the title deed of the earth to John and instruct him to eat it. This will symbolize mankind's legal inheritance to the earth. By eating it and finding it to be bitter in his stomach, John will exemplify that the possession of the world is sweet, but the events that lead up to this moment will cause great sorrow to the human race.[10]

What this means is that people usually feel pleasure in being able to see or be foretold future events by receiving a word from God, whatever it may be. However, as Bible scholar Matthew Henry explains, "...when this book of prophecy was more thoroughly digested by the apostle [John], the contents would be bitter; these were things so awful and terrible, such grievous persecutions of the people of God, and such desolation made in the earth, that the foresight and fore-knowledge of them would not be pleasant, but painful to the mind of the apostle...." [11]

THE TWO WITNESSES RAPTURED

The Antichrist will observe as his empire crumbles. In his fury, he will attack those who have attacked him—particularly the two witnesses we saw earlier. He will kill them in Jerusalem and leave their bodies lying on the street for all the world to see. This will last for three and a half days for the world to observe.

> And when they shall have finished their testimony, the beast that ascendeth out of the bottomless pit shall make war against them, and shall overcome them, and kill them.
>
> And their dead bodies shall lie in the street of the great city, which spiritually is called Sodom and Egypt, where also our Lord was crucified.
>
> And they of the people and kindreds and tongues and nations shall see their dead bodies three days and an half, and shall not suffer their dead bodies to be put in graves.
>
> And they that dwell upon the earth shall rejoice over them, and make merry, and shall send gifts one to another; because these two prophets tormented them that dwelt on the earth.
>
> Revelation 11:7-10

As people watch these events unfold on television, they will rejoice at the death of the two witnesses because their praying, preaching, and courage in persecution will have caused many to feel self-condemned and scared stiff. However, more will be amazed as the witnesses resurrect and ascend into heaven.

> And after three days and an half the Spirit of life from God entered into them, and they stood upon their feet; and great fear fell upon them which saw them.
>
> And they heard a great voice from heaven saying unto them, Come up hither. And they ascended up to heaven in a cloud; and their enemies beheld them.
>
> Revelation 11:11,12

During the two witnesses' rapture, an earthquake in Jerusalem will kill 7,000 of the city's inhabitants.

> And the same hour was there a great earthquake, and the tenth part of the city fell, and in the earthquake were slain of men seven thousand: and the remnant were affrighted, and gave glory to the God of heaven.
>
> Revelation 11:13

To see this incredible event of the two witnesses' resurrection and its aftermath of destruction on earth will stun those left in that evil day. They will be so amazed, convicted, and terrified that for the moment they will acknowledge that the power of God is in it all.

Now the stage will finally be set for Armageddon.

CHAPTER 13

A WAR WITHOUT FIGHTING

No other aspect of the end times is as misunderstood as Armageddon. While it strikes fear in the hearts of some, to others, the word *Armageddon* has become nothing more than a term signifying the struggle between good and evil,[1] or a bloody battle. Used to describe the destruction of the world and the end of humankind, Armageddon has been called a war without winners.

Armageddon is the final rebellion of Satan and man against God. It will be a terrible battle that will create a river of blood. But, in one sense, it will be a war without fighting.

The Antichrist will gather a global army, pillaging cities and killing thousands. Not once, however, will Satan and his servants lift a sword against the Lord. When Christ returns with His bride to earth, Satan's army will be destroyed with the voice of our Savior.[2] Therefore, there will be no real struggle between good and evil because Christ will overcome without lifting a finger.

The word *Armageddon*—originally the Greek word *Oar-mageddwvn*[3]—is not found in the Septuagint[4] and appears only once in the Bible in the book of Revelation:

> For they are the spirits of devils, working miracles, which go forth unto the kings of the earth and of the whole world, to gather them to the battle of that great day of God Almighty.

> And he gathered them together into a place called in the Hebrew tongue Armageddon.
>
> Revelation 16:14,16

The term *Apocalypse* is often associated with this last great battle, Armageddon, and is actually the Greek word for *Revelation*. It is defined as "...one of the Jewish and Christian writings of 200 B.C. to A.D. 150 marked by...the expectation of an imminent cosmic cataclysm in which God destroys the ruling powers of evil and raises the righteous to life in a messianic kingdom."[5] *Cataclysm* refers to an event that brings about great change. The Battle of Armageddon will change the world forever.

Armageddon seems to be formed from the Hebrew word, *Har Megiddo*—the mountain or hill of Megiddo.[6] The city of Megiddo, which is in the northern part of present-day Israel, is named after this mountain, or hill.

In 2 Chronicles 35:22, the Bible says that Josiah "...came to fight in the valley of Megiddo." Megiddo was a town belonging to Manasseh, although within the limits of Issachar.[7] It had been originally one of the royal cities of the Canaanites and was one of those cities that was unable to be taken over by the Israelites for a long time.[8] Eventually it was rebuilt and fortified by Solomon.

> And this is the reason of the levy which king Solomon raised; for to build the house of the Lord, and his own house, and Millo, and the wall of Jerusalem, and Hazor, and Megiddo, and Gezer.
>
> 1 Kings 9:15

It is the city that Ahaziah, king of Judah, fled to when wounded by Jehu and where Ahaziah later died.

> But when Ahaziah the king of Judah saw this, he fled by the way of the garden house. And Jehu followed after him, and said, Smite him also in the chariot. And they did so at the going up to Gur, which is by Ibleam. And he fled to Megiddo, and died there.
>
> 2 Kings 9:27

One Bible source describes the location of Megiddo, saying, "...It has not been found easy to identify the place, but recent searches have made it probable that the vale [valley] or plain of Megiddo comprehended, if it was not wholly composed of, the prolongation of the plain of Esdra-elon towards Mount Carmel; that the city of Megiddo was situated there; and that the waters of Megiddo, mentioned in Judges 5:19, are identical with the stream Kishon in that part of its course...."[9]

This vale or valley of Megiddo, called the Jezreel Valley, served as the location for several famous battles in the Old Testament, including Barak over the Canaanites and Gideon over the Midianites.

Another interesting fact about this valley is that two great disasters took place here—the deaths of Saul and Josiah.

In the book of Revelation, it is described as "a place of great slaughter," and "the scene of a terrible retribution upon the wicked."[10] It is in this valley that many scholars believe the Battle of Armageddon will take place.

THE GATHERING PLACE

I've visited Megiddo fourteen times, and I always find this area awesome as I look down from the ruins of King Solomon's once-magnificent horse stables into the Valley of Jezreel (which is what the Israelis call the area today).

The Valley of Jezreel is a fertile, lush valley where grapes, cabbages, barley, and potatoes grow in abundance. The nation of Israel is fed with these crops. It is a calm place, where the morning sunshine chases away the mists of the Kishon River Valley.

Before the Israelis turned this area into the nation's bread-basket in the 1950s, it was primarily a swamp. The area is so flat that the Kishon River runs slowly through the valley. When rains came in the spring, the valley would flood and leave the land in standing water for several months. But with new flood-control systems, the land is kept clear for farming. It took a great deal of time and hard work to turn this swampland into farmland.

It's hard to believe that this serene setting has been the site of countless battles in history and will be the gathering place for Satan's monstrous army at the end of the Tribulation. But, in fact, in Hebrew, the word *Megiddo* also means "place of crowds,"[11] or assembly, and "rendezvous."[12] It is derived from *gadad*, which means to "crowd, assemble selves by troops."[13] Its name is well suited, for the valley of Megiddo boasts a rich military history (and future).

At one time it was one of the capital cities of the Canaanites. The Egyptian king Thothmes III is said to have commented that "Megiddo is worth a thousand cities." Location is the reason. Megiddo sits on the pass that leads through Mount Carmel to the Mediterranean. This is considered to be one of the most strategic crossroads in Palestine—anyone wishing to control the Middle East would need to control the vital trade and military routes connecting Europe, Africa, and Asia.[14]

According to some historical accounts, Napoleon stood looking out over Megiddo before the famous battle that kept him from conquering the East and rebuilding the Roman Empire. Reflecting upon the immensity of the plain of Armageddon, he declared, "All the armies of the world could maneuver their forces on this vast plain."[15]

This valley, which is 55 miles northwest of Jerusalem, was the crossroads of two ancient trade routes: one leading from the Mediterranean Sea on the west to the Jordan River valley on the east, the other leading from Syria, Phoenicia, and Galilee in the north to the hill country of Judah and the land of Egypt on the south.

This triangular plain is 300 square miles and is bordered on the southwest by the Carmel Mountain range and on the north by the hills of Nazareth. It contains rich farmland because of the soil washed down into it from the mountains of Galilee and the highlands of Samaria. It is also the only east-west valley that divides the mountain ranges of western Palestine.

The valley lies at the entrance to a pass across the Carmel Mountain range on the main highway between Asia and Africa. It is the key position between the Euphrates and Nile rivers. And, remember, it was a strategic military site and the scene of many ancient battles, many of which were fought by the people of Israel.

CANAANITE KINGS

Yet the children of Manasseh could not drive out the inhabitants of those cities; but the Canaanites would dwell in that land.

Yet it came to pass, when the children of Israel were waxen strong, that they put the Canaanites to tribute; but did not utterly drive them out.

And the children of Joseph spake unto Joshua, saying, Why hast thou given me but one lot and one portion to inherit, seeing I am a great people, forasmuch as the Lord hath blessed me hitherto?

And Joshua answered them, If thou be a great people, then get thee up to the wood country, and cut down for thyself there in the land of the Perizzites and of the giants, if mount Ephraim be too narrow for thee.

And the children of Joseph said, The hill is not enough for us: and all the Canaanites that dwell in the land of the valley have chariots of iron, both they who are of Bethshean and her towns, and they who are of the valley of Jezreel.

And Joshua spake unto the house of Joseph, even to Ephraim and to Manasseh, saying, Thou art a great people, and hast great power: thou shalt not have one lot only:

But the mountain shall be thine; for it is a wood, and thou shalt cut it down: and the outgoings of it shall be thine: for thou shalt drive out the Canaanites, though they have iron chariots, and though they be strong.

Joshua 17:12-18

The king of Megiddo was one of thirty-one Canaanite kings whom Joshua and the Israelites conquered in order to claim the Promised Land.[16] The land then became the possession of the tribe of Manasseh, but the people were afraid to drive out the Canaanites who lived there because they had chariots of iron.

AHAZIAH, KING OF JUDAH

But when Ahaziah the king of Judah saw this, he fled by the way of the garden house. And Jehu followed after him, and said, Smite him also in the chariot. And they did so at the going up to Gur, which is by Ibleam. And he fled to Megiddo, and died there.

2 Kings 9:27

Ahaziah, king of Judah, was attacked on the way to Gur when he fled Jehu and then died in Megiddo.

KING AHAB

All the people associated with King Ahab's reign, including Jezebel, were assassinated by the followers of Jehu in the Valley of Jezreel.[17]

PHILISTINES AND KING SAUL

Now the Philistines fought against Israel: and the men of Israel fled from before the Philistines, and fell down slain in mount Gilboa.

And the Philistines followed hard upon Saul and upon his sons; and the Philistines slew Jonathan, and Abinadab, and Malchishua, Saul's sons.

And the battle went sore against Saul, and the archers hit him; and he was sore wounded of the archers.

1 Samuel 31:1-3

The Philistines were victorious over King Saul at Megiddo.

THE EGYPTIANS AND JOSIAH

In his days Pharaoh-nechoh king of Egypt went up against the king of Assyria to the river Euphrates: and king Josiah went against him; and he slew him at Megiddo, when he had seen him.

2 Kings 23:29

The Egyptians mortally wounded Josiah, king of Judah, when he attempted to intercept the army of Pharaoh-nechoh in the valley.

DEBORAH AND BARAK

The kings came and fought, then fought the kings of Canaan in Taanach by the waters of Megiddo; they took no gain of money.

Judges 5:19

During the judges period, the forces of Deborah and Barak wiped out the army of Sisera in the swampy riverbanks of the Kishon River. And the kings of Canaan who fought against Israel for repossession of the land were defeated in Maanach on the river's edge.[18]

INCREDIBLE GRACE AND MERCY

The last great battle, the Battle of Armageddon, will take place in this valley. I believe that the reason this battle will be so devastating is that God's patience will culminate to where He can no longer tolerate man's sins.

But even in the midst of the outpouring of His wrath, God will still show incredible grace and mercy on people who turn from their sins and receive Christ as their Redeemer. That's why Jesus encourages us when He says, "But he that shall endure unto the end, the same shall be saved" (Matt. 24:13).

WAR WITH ISRAEL

And he gathered them together into a place called m the Hebrew tongue Armageddon.

Revelation 16:16

In the last chapter we saw that the fury of the Antichrist will be kindled by the resurrection and ascension of the two witnesses. They made a fool of him, and, in retribution, he will decide to take his campaign against God and His people to the ultimate level. He will declare war on Israel and assemble his confederate armies in Armageddon.

Joel 2:2 says that this army of the devil is like "...a great people and a strong; there hath not been ever the like, neither shall be any more after it...." So many soldiers will be in this invading force that the sun will be blocked by the dust they kick up.

Joel compares this multitude to the huge locust swarms of his day. Thousands upon thousands of locusts would come over the plains and mountains and block out the light of the sun. Their approach could be heard for miles. People knew with the locusts came destruction. They realized there was nothing they could do to prevent their coming. It will be very similar with the enormous army the Antichrist will gather together.

THEY'RE COMING!

Likewise, the people will see and hear the coming of the Antichrist's army as they head east out of Armageddon and south down the Jordan River Valley. When they arrive at Jericho, they will turn west towards Jerusalem.

In distress, the people will sound the alarm. They will blow the ram's horn, called a shofar. This is the instrument that was blown by the Israelites before battles. The horn makes low, guttural music, calling the people to arm themselves and prepare to fight.

As the people prepare for this Battle of Armageddon, the Israelites must arm themselves ingenuously. During the last three and a half years, they have faced natural disasters, demonic attacks, and persecution from the Antichrist. Only a handful of guns, grenades, and other weapons will remain after all the destruction and weapons confiscation.

I believe that they will make weapons out of wood and other available materials. I imagine they will create spears, bows and arrows, and "Molotov cocktails" (bombs made out of bottles and flammable liquids such as alcohol).

Can you picture their terrified faces as they hear the Antichrist's army marching through Israel? Isaiah foretold these terrible events in his prophetic book:

> He is come to Aiath, he is passed to Migron; at Michmash he hath laid up his carriages:
>
> They are gone over the passage: they have taken up their lodging at Geba; Ramah is afraid; Gibeah of Saul is fled.
>
> Lift up thy voice, O daughter of Gallim: cause it to be heard unto Laish, O poor Anathoth.
>
> Madmenah is removed; the inhabitants of Gebim gather themselves to flee.
>
> As yet shall he remain at Nob that day: he shall shake his hand against the mount of the daughter of Zion, the hill of Jerusalem.
>
> Behold, the Lord, the Lord of hosts, shall lop the bough with terror: and the high ones of stature shall be hewn down, and the haughty shall be humbled.
>
> And he shall cut down the thickets of the forest with iron, and Lebanon shall fall by a mighty one.
>
> Isaiah 10:28-34

Just envision the scene: The roar of the soldiers' marching, their machines, and their destructions will echo through the air like thunder. The explosions they set off behind them will ignite the sky like lightning.

Joel 2:3 says, "A fire devoureth before them; and behind them a flame burneth ...." So intent will they be on destruction that the armies of the Antichrist will set off bombs, including chemical, biological, and other deadly weapons, to turn the land of Israel into a "desolate wilderness." Their bombs will sound and look like "the noise of a flame of fire" (Joel 2:5). These weapons will set Israel ablaze.

A DISCIPLINED FIGHTING MACHINE

We can certainly see that this army is like no other. Nuclear weapons will be the prime choice for destruction. No thought will be given to conquering the country or protecting anyone's life or property. The intent of the devil and his army will be to annihilate Israel and God's people. Generals will not weep when their battalions fall due to explosions and radiation; they will push on and keep their eyes on the prize of Jerusalem's destruction.

Although it would be easier for the Antichrist to destroy Israel by simply launching a nuclear weapon into the country, I believe that he will not be able to do this. Logic would dictate that it is likely the massive destruction to the earth by the seven seals will destroy most, if not all, of the military's advanced technology, including missile launchers, radar systems, and more. Armies (not just the defenders in Jerusalem) will have to use whatever is handy to fight with, including turning farm implements into weapons of war.

Beat your plowshares into swords, and your pruning-hooks into spears: let the weak say, I am strong.

Joel 3:10

Although the technology will no longer be available to launch the missiles, the nuclear warheads will still be intact. Most likely, they will have been protected in subterranean silos. The Antichrist will have the machinery of destruction available, but he will be forced to bring it to his target on foot.

The appearance of them is as the appearance of horses; and as horsemen, so shall they run.

Joel 2:4

The Antichrist's army will be extremely agile. He will use horses and maybe even tanks and other armored vehicles to help them move with unity and precision through the valleys, mountains, and rough terrain of Israel. They will not break their ranks and will be extremely precise.

They shall run like mighty men; they shall climb the wall like men of war; and they shall march every one on his ways, and they shall not break their ranks:

Joel 2:7

Satan's force will be the most disciplined fighting machine the world has ever witnessed.

"Neither shall one thrust another."

Joel 2:8

In Hebrew, this phrase says that the soldiers do not press the other, meaning they are extremely disciplined and trained.[19] This will be no hodgepodge attack; it will be well coordinated and organized. Every man will march in unison with the other. No one will seek attention or praise. They will have a common goal and present a united front against God.

Another phrase in Joel 2:8 provides insight into the army: "And when they fall upon the sword, they shall not be wounded." The NIV Bible translation of this verse actually says, "They plunge through defenses without breaking ranks." I have no doubt in my mind that Satan will give his men incredible strength and agility, but he will not be able to keep them from dying. He will have too many soldiers to care about the lives of a few thousand men, so there will be no need to protect them.

Some other Bible translations of Joel 2:8 describe Satan's army like this:

> ...When they burst through the defenses, they do not *break ranks.*
>
> Joel 2:8 NASB

> Neither doth one thrust another; they march every one in his path; and they burst through the weapons, and *break not off their course.*
>
> Joel 2:8 ASV

The bottom line is, this army will be so coordinated that they will march forward as one person—nothing will be able to stop them or the horrors they inflict.

EVIL BATTLE PLAN

When the armies finally arrive in Jerusalem, they will attack ruthlessly. The soldiers will rush on the city and climb the walls, beginning the work of war: "They shall run to and fro in the city...they shall climb up upon the houses, they shall enter in at the windows like a thief" (Joel 2:9). They will ransack, rob, plunder, strip bare the houses, rape the women, and take half the people into captivity.

All along the way they will be raping and pillaging before they destroy the villages and towns of Israel as part of the devil's plan to torture God's people.

> For I will gather all nations against Jerusalem to battle; and the city shall be taken, and the houses rifled, and the women ravished; and half of the city shall go forth into captivity, and the residue of the people shall not be cut off from the city.
>
> Zechariah 14:2

The people in Jerusalem will react with fear and horror and will be in tremendous pain and anguish.

> Before their face the people shall be much pained: all faces shall gather blackness.
>
> Joel 2:6

This army will be worse than any thing they could imagine, causing their faces to "gather blackness." That means they will turn pale with anxiety and fright as they realize the enormity and fierceness of the army that has come to attack them.

FINAL WAKE-UP CALL

When the soldiers are through looting and attacking, they will leave the city and gather in the Valley of Jehoshaphat. Remember, it is part of the Kidron Valley on the east side of the city between the Temple and the Mount of Olives. The Antichrist will have prepared his nuclear weapons and the troops will assemble to leave the area so he can detonate the devices.

The army will think it is following the commands of their demon-general to gather in this valley. But it will actually be following God's plan, who will call the army into "the valley of Jehoshaphat" in order to deal with and judge them. (The name *Jehoshaphat* means "Jehovah-judged."[20])

> Let the heathen be wakened, and come up to the valley of Jehoshaphat: for there will I sit to judge all the heathen round about.
>
> Joel 3:12

When they get into the valley, every thing will become pitch black. God will darken the sun and moon and stop the stars from shining for 24 hours.

> The sun and the moon shall be darkened, and the stars shall withdraw their shining.
>
> Joel 3:15

> It shall come to pass in that day, *that* the light shall not be clear, *nor* dark:
>
> Zechariah 14:6

It will be as if time stands still. Their machinery will not work, and they will not be able to see to march or walk. Each soldier will be forced to remain where he stands.

God calls the Valley of Jehoshaphat the "valley of decision" in Joel 3:14, because during the 24 hours of inactivity and calm, God will give the nations of the world one final opportunity to repent of their sins. As we saw in Joel 3:12, it will be His final "wake-up call" to their spirits.

Throughout time, God has always shown people His character. He has revealed His glory through nature, the stars, the miracles of life, His Word, and His people. Remember that during the Tribulation, He will send angels to witness, have 144,000 Jewish people tell His story, give the two witnesses the power to work miracles, and send supernatural judgments. Even after all of that, God will still give the people who reject Him and rebel against His love and authority one more opportunity to change their minds. In fact, He will give them the peace and quiet they need to think clearly about their situation because God does not send His judgment on anyone until He has first shown His mercy.

During this same 24 hours, God will deal with the people who remain in Jerusalem. Many will still be alive, but they will be bleeding, beaten, and frightened. When the darkness descends, I believe they will wonder what kind of trouble has befallen them again. But then they will hear the Lord speak to them, saying, "...turn ye even to me with all your heart, and with fasting, and with weeping, and with mourning: And rend your heart, and not your garments, and turn unto the Lord your God: for he is gracious and merciful, slow to anger, and of great kindness, and repenteth him of the evil" (Joel 2:12,13).

TRUE REPENTANCE

I think that this call to repentance is very beautiful and typical of God. For centuries, the Jews have rejected God in so many ways. We can see in the Bible that at the very beginning of their nation, they worshiped golden calves, brazen idols, and hateful false gods of heathen nations. Even though they had received the most powerful demonstrations of God's love and mercy, they still doubted and refused His Presence.

They later will reject their true Messiah but accept a heinous lie of the devil, the Antichrist, as their "savior." In choosing Satan's lies of physical peace and prosperity, they will show God that His promise of inner peace and soul prosperity is not good enough.

Through it all, however, God's anger against them was, and will be, slow to boil. His every step, judgment, and sign through the ages has been given to show them the truth of who He is and who they are in Him. He never gave up on them, returning repeatedly to purchase them from the pit of their sins. And in the end times, He will do the same.

His final attempt to obtain the Jews' attention will be very loving. He will speak to them in the darkness and tell them, "Today is the day of your salvation." Their situation couldn't be worse; but as we just saw in Joel 2:12-13, in the midst of it all, God will talk to them, wooing them into the safety of His arms.

He desires for them to give Him their hearts and to show repentance through fasting, weeping, and praying. They cannot truly repent and accept the Lord's sacrifice without some sort of outward evidence of their changed natures.

Even if they do not show their emotions, God wants them to break their hearts in repentance. People who only make the outward show of tearing their garments are not saved; God chooses those who break their hearts in true repentance to be His own.

Sometimes people "go through the motions" of repenting but do not mean it.

Cain and Abel both offered sacrifices for their sins, but one gave with a broken heart (Abel) and the other gave as an act of responsibility (Cain). For this reason, God accepted Abel's sacrifice of repentance but rejected Cain's.[21]

From this example you can see the difference in the meanings of the word *repent*. Jesus told the people to "...Repent: for the kingdom of heaven is at hand" (Matt. 4:17). In this verse, "repent" is the Greek word *metanoeo*, which means "to think differently...."[22] Jesus was calling people to change their lives by changing their mind or attitude. This is true repentance.

However, when Judas "repented himself" after he betrayed Christ, he had a change of emotion. (Matt. 27:3.) The word "repent" here is the Greek word *metamellomai*, which means "to care afterwards...."[23] Judas was remorseful, but he didn't change his heart or his life. This is repentance in name only.

> Blow the trumpet in Zion, sanctify a fast, call a solemn assembly:
>
> Gather the people, sanctify the congregation, assemble the elders, gather the children, and those that suck the breasts: let the bridegroom go forth of his chamber, and the bride out of her closet.

> Let the priests, the ministers of the Lord, weep between the porch and the altar, and let them say, Spare thy people, O Lord, and give not thine heritage to reproach, that the heathen should rule over them: wherefore should they say among the people, Where is their God?
>
> Joel 2:15-17

When the Jews accept God's call and ask for His help, they will blow the trumpet, sanctify a fast, and call a solemn assembly. The priests will weep to the Lord in intercession for the people. They will accept Jesus' sacrifice and beg Him to return quickly.

> The Lord also shall roar out of Zion, and utter his voice from Jerusalem; and the heavens and the earth shall shake: but the Lord will be the hope of his people, and the strength of the children of Israel.
>
> So shall ye know that I am the Lord your God dwelling in Zion, my holy mountain: then shall Jerusalem be holy, and there shall no strangers pass through her any more.
>
> Joel 3:16,17

When the Jews repent at the Battle of Armageddon, God promises to be gracious and merciful to them. He will forgive them of their sins and protect them. God will offer His people the solution to this and every problem they have. In this time of distress, God will help them because they will turn to Him and ask for help. This conversion of the Jews will solemnize the marriage between Jesus and His bride, the church.[24]

SECTION 5

THE
MILLENNIUM

CHAPTER 14

RESCUE AND DEFEAT

While all we've covered so far is happening on earth, a great event will be unfolding in heaven—the Marriage Supper of the Lamb.[1] The saints and angels will gather to witness this awesome event.

The bride of Christ will be arrayed in the linen of righteousness, washed clean and white by the blood of the Lamb.[2] The bride will include all the believers who awaited His first coming, those who accepted Him after His death and resurrection, and the ones who asked Him into their hearts during the Tribulation.

Christ will enter the chapel on a white horse. His eyes will be as a flame of fire, and many crowns will be on His head. His robe will be dipped in blood.[3]

And here is the mind which hath wisdom. The seven heads are seven mountains, on which the woman sitteth.

And there are seven kings: five are fallen, and one is, and the other is not yet come; and when he cometh, he must continue a short space.

And the beast that was, and is not, even he is the eighth, and is of the seven, and goeth into perdition.

And the ten horns which thou sawest are ten kings, which have received no kingdom as yet; but receive power as kings one hour with the beast.

These have one mind, and shall give their power and strength unto the beast.

These shall make war with the Lamb, and the Lamb shall overcome them: for he is Lord of lords, and King of kings: and they that are with him are called, and chosen, and faithful.

Revelation 17:9-14

As this passage indicates, the ceremony is a call to war. When it is finished, His saints will mount white horses to follow Him and be part of Satan's ultimate defeat.[4]

CHRIST'S RETURN

God will respond to the trumpet call of His people in Jerusalem, and He will order the seventh trumpet to be blown in heaven. With a "roar out of Zion," Jesus will return with His army, His bride.

The Lord also shall roar out of Zion, and utter his voice from Jerusalem; and the heavens and the earth shall shake: but the Lord will be the hope of his people, and the strength of the children of Israel.

Joel 3:16

The army of the Antichrist will not turn to Jesus while in the valley of decision. God will judge their choice, and they will be sentenced to death and eternal damnation. Jesus' war cry (the Word of God) will become the Sword of the Lord and slay the Antichrist's army. Their blood will flow in a river 200 miles long and four feet deep.

> And the winepress was trodden without the city, and blood came out of the winepress, even unto the horse bridles, by the space of a thousand *and* six hundred furlongs.
>
> Revelation 14:20

I believe that this river of blood will flow in the Jordan River Valley, which is 200 miles long from the Sea of Galilee to the area south of the Dead Sea.

This battle will be the harvest in which Jesus separates the wheat from the chaff.

> Whose fan is in his hand, and he will throughly purge his floor, and gather his wheat into the garner; but he will burn up the chaff with unquenchable fire.
>
> Matthew 3:12

The chaff, representing the wicked, will blow away to the place of unquenchable fire, which symbolizes the eternal suffering of the wicked in hell.[5] But the wheat, representing the righteous, or the people of God, will remain and become the bread of life that blesses the earth during the Millennium.

Nature will respond to Christ's return with lightning, thunder, 60-pound hail, and an earthquake that shakes the world. Let's look at some Scriptures that describe all of this.

But the Lord is the true God, he is the living God, and an everlasting king: at his wrath *the earth shall tremble,* and the nations shall not be able to abide his indignation.

Jeremiah 10:10

Immediately after the tribulation of those days shall *the sun be darkened, and the moon shall not give her light, and the stars shall fall from heaven,* and the powers of the heavens shall be shaken:

And then shall appear the sign of the Son of man in heaven: and then shall all the tribes of the earth mourn, and they shall see the Son of man coming in the clouds of heaven with power and great glory.

And he shall send his angels with a great sound of a trumpet, and they shall gather together his elect from the four winds, from one end of heaven to the other.

Matthew 24:29-31

And there shall be signs in the sun, and in the moon, and in the stars; and upon the earth distress of nations, with perplexity; the sea and the waves roaring;

Men's hearts failing them for fear, and for looking after those things which are coming on the earth: for the powers of heaven shall be shaken.

And then shall they see the Son of man coming in a cloud with power and great glory.

Luke 21:25-27

And the nations were angry, and thy wrath is come, and the time of the dead, that they should be judged, and that thou shouldest give reward unto thy servants the prophets, and to the saints, and them that fear thy name, small and great; and shouldest destroy them which destroy the earth.

And the temple of God was opened in heaven, and there was seen in his temple the ark of his testament: and *there were lightnings, and voices, and thunderings, and an earthquake, and great hail.*

Revelation 11:18,19

And the seventh angel poured out his vial into the air; and there came a great voice out of the temple of heaven, from the throne, saying, It is done.

And there were *voices, and thunders, and lightnings; and there was a great earthquake,* such as was not since men were upon the earth, so mighty an earthquake, and so great.

And the great city was divided into three parts, and the cities of the nations fell: and great Babylon came in remembrance before God, to give unto her the cup of the wine of the fierceness of his wrath.

And *every island fled away, and the mountains were not found.*

And *there fell upon men a great hail out of heaven, every stone about the weight of a talent:* and men blasphemed God because of the plague of the hail; for the plague thereof was exceeding great.

Revelation 16:17-21

Islands and mountains will move, and entire countries and cities will be destroyed, including Egypt and Edom (an area which was southeast of the Dead Sea in ancient times).[6]

> Egypt shall be a desolation, and Edom shall be a desolate
> wilderness, for the violence against the children of Judah,
> because they have shed innocent blood in their land.
>
> Joel 3:19

Babylon will receive the full brunt of God's wrath as He destroys it with fire coming from heaven and an explosion in the earth. This is the same way Sodom and Gomorrah were destroyed.[7]

Babylon will fall in a day. No one will survive, and according to Scripture, no one will ever live in the city again.

> It shall never be inhabited, neither shall it be dwelt in from generation to generation: neither shall the Arabian pitch tent there; neither shall the shepherds make their fold there.
>
> But wild beasts of the desert shall lie there; and their houses shall be full of doleful creatures; and owls shall dwell there, and satyrs shall dance there.
>
> Isaiah 13:20,21

> Reward her even as she rewarded you, and double unto her double according to her works: in the cup which she hath filled fill to her double.
>
> How much she hath glorified herself, and lived deliciously, so much torment and sorrow give her: for she saith in her heart, I sit a queen, and am no widow, and shall see no sorrow.
>
> Therefore shall her plagues come in one day, death, and mourning, and famine; and she shall be utterly burned with fire: for strong is the Lord God who judgeth her.
>
> Revelation 18:6-8

This passage leads me to believe that the bomb intended for Jerusalem instead will level Babylon.

> And the ten horns which thou sawest upon the beast, these shall hate the whore, and shall make her desolate and naked, and shall eat her flesh, and burn her with fire.

> For God hath put in their hearts to fulfil his will, and to agree, and give their kingdom unto the beast, until the words of God shall be fulfilled.
>
> Revelation 17:16,17

This destruction of Babylon also will be a judgment of cults, false religions, and idolatry. Remember, all of these were pictured as the whore of Revelation 17. With the return of Christ, the nations will realize the whore's deception and destroy her once and for all.

FOREVER CHANGED

Jerusalem will change dramatically at the Second Coming. When Jesus' feet touch the Mount of Olives, the mountain will rip in two all the way from the Mediterranean to the Dead Sea, which is 1,200 feet below sea level. The waters of the Mediterranean will rush into the Dead Sea, carrying with it many of the dead soldiers whose bodies are scattered over the countryside. This new river will flow from Jerusalem, which has been divided into three parts.

> And his feet shall stand in that day upon the mount of Olives, which is before Jerusalem on the east, and the mount of Olives shall cleave in the midst thereof toward the east and toward the west, and there shall be a very

great valley; and half of the mountain shall remove toward the north, and half of it toward the south.

And it shall be in that day, that living waters shall go out from Jerusalem; half of them toward the former sea, and half of them toward the hinder sea: in summer and in winter shall it be.

Zechariah 14:4,8

And the great city was divided into three parts, and the cities of the nations fell: and great Babylon came in remembrance before God, to give unto her the cup of the wine of the fierceness of his wrath.

Revelation 16:19

An angel will invite flesh-eating birds to the "supper of the great God," a term which suggests there will be a great slaughter of God's enemies.[8] These birds will feast on the bodies of the dead soldiers.

And I saw an angel standing in the sun; and he cried with a loud voice, saying to all the fowls that fly in the midst of heaven, Come and gather yourselves together unto the supper of the great God;

That ye may eat the flesh of kings, and the flesh of captains, and the flesh of mighty men, and the flesh of horses, and of them that sit on them, and the flesh of all men, both free and bond, both small and great.

Revelation 19:17,18

In the midst of all this, the smell of decaying flesh will saturate the air.

But I will remove far off from you the northern army, and will drive him into a land barren and desolate, with his face toward the east sea, and his hinder part toward the utmost sea, and his stink shall come up, and his ill savour shall come up, because he hath done great things.

Joel 2:20

One of the best outcomes of the Battle of Armageddon is that the Antichrist and False Prophet will be thrown into the Lake of Fire to be persecuted forever, Satan will be chained in the bottomless pit for 1,000 years, and his demons will be expelled from earth.[9]

I get passionate about the terrorism that is going on around the world. Terrorism is a hideous thing, but as bad as world terrorism is, the devil's terrorism in the final battle on the earth will be even worse. Yet God will absolutely break the back of darkness and have total victory. He will put an end to Satan's evil plans and halt his darkest and most dangerous terrorist attacks. And the high point will be that Christ will take possession of the earth and walk in victory through the eastern gate of His capital city, Jerusalem. His 1,000-year reign of the world will begin!

NEW BEGINNINGS

...It is done.

Revelation 16:17

When the smoke clears and the rumblings of the earth are silenced, the redeemed in Jerusalem will look out of their walled city to see the countryside and mountains of Israel

covered with the dead bodies of soldiers and their horses—
hundreds of thousands of them—while vultures will circle
and land on the bodies for this great "feast."[10]

All the people of Israel and travelers who pass through
the land will spend the next seven months burying the dead.
The valley where they will bury the Antichrist's army is just
east of the Mediterranean. They will rename it the Valley of
Hamon-gog, which means "the multitude of Gog,"[11] who is
the Antichrist.

> And it shall come to pass in that day, that I will give unto
> Gog a place there of graves in Israel, the valley of the pas-
> sengers on the east of the sea: and it shall stop the noses of
> the passengers: and there shall they bury Gog and all his
> multitude: and they shall call it The valley of Hamongog.
>
> And seven months shall the house of Israel be burying of
> them, that they may cleanse the land.
>
> Yea, all the people of the land shall bury them; and it shall
> be to them a renown the day that I shall be glorified, saith
> the Lord God.
>
> And they shall sever out men of continual employment,
> passing through the land to bury with the passengers
> those that remain upon the face of the earth, to cleanse it:
> after the end of seven months shall they search.
>
> And the passengers that pass through the land, when any
> seeth a man's bone, then shall he set up a sign by it, till the
> buriers have buried it in the valley of Hamongog.
>
> And also the name of the city shall be Hamonah. Thus
> shall they cleanse the land.
>
> Ezekiel 39:11-16

People will go through the land, gathering their own weapons and those of the Antichrist's fallen army to use as fuel for their stoves and fireplaces. They will use the spears, guns, and ammunition instead of wood, allowing the earth to recover and replenish itself after the seven years of destruction in the Tribulation.[12]

Men and women will no longer be able to look to the works of their hands or the beauty of their world to bring them contentment or joy. They will no longer be all-powerful or in control. Because of the state of the world, they will be completely reliant upon God.

The plagues, earthquakes, hail, and fire will have destroyed man's churches, temples, mosques, and altars. Man's buildings, paintings, sculptures, and other creations will have been obliterated. The places people used to go to experience nature's beauty will be gone. Their earth will be smoking, boiling, and in ruins. But Armageddon will not mark the end of humanity.

I'm convinced that the greatest days are ahead and that what God is going to do with this earth and His people at that time will be pure "dynamite."

Under Christ's supervision, and with the saints' help, people of the earth will begin the reconstruction of their homes. They will cleanse the earth of the dead, plant their fields, and clothe their bodies.

God's righteous—Christians and all the Jews who believe Jesus is their Messiah—will receive the title deed to the earth. They will live without evil in their midst and will be part of the divine process of restoring this world into the paradise it was before man's fall from grace.

In bodies that will not die and with hearts that won't break, mankind will begin an eternity of praise and fellowship with our Father, our Savior, the Holy Spirit, and our brethren in Christ. This extraordinary time will mark the start of new beginnings that will be filled with the greatest days we've ever known on earth.

CHAPTER 15

RESTORATION AND REGENERATION

M any people have taught that the Millennium will be a perfect time on this earth when humans receive glorified bodies and renewed minds, and nature is redeemed from its curse. I believe that this is a misconception; the Millennium will be a time of perfecting this world and its inhabitants, not of living in perfection. (The only people who will live in glorified bodies will be the saints who were raptured or resurrected before or during the Tribulation.)

We just saw some of what will happen during the Millennium according to the Word: Bodies will need to be buried, things will stink, people will need to find ways to keep warm, and employment will be necessary.[1] Furthermore, the laws of nature will remain somewhat unchanged because, while the world will carry some old curses, new blessings will begin to take shape.

Living waters will spring from the house of the Lord— the temple—and flow southward out of Jerusalem until the river breaks into two branches, one that travels to the

Mediterranean Sea and the other to the Dead Sea. This was foretold in the Old Testament:

> Afterward he brought me again unto the door of the house; and, behold, waters issued out from under the threshold of the house eastward: for the forefront of the house stood toward the east, and the waters came down from under from the right side of the house, at the south side of the altar.
>
> Ezekiel 47:1

> And it shall come to pass in that day, that the mountains shall drop down new wine, and the hills shall flow with milk, and all the rivers of Judah shall flow with waters, and a fountain shall come forth of the house of the Lord, and shall water the valley of Shittim.
>
> Joel 3:18

> And it shall be in that day, that living waters shall go out from Jerusalem; half of them toward the former sea, and half of them toward the hinder sea: in summer and in winter shall it be.
>
> Zechariah 14:8

Clarke's Commentary gives a wonderful description of the spiritual meaning of these living waters: " ...a wide diffusion of divine knowledge, and of the plan of human salvation...shall go out by apostles and preachers, first from Jerusalem, then to Syria, Asia Minor, Greece, Italy, the isles of the sea, Britain, etc....in the countries where there was no knowledge of God, there shall these waters flow. The stream shall never cease; it shall run in summer as well as winter. These are living waters— perennial, incessant; and waters that shall preserve life."[2]

In the natural, this river will affect the land so there will be no drought but an abundance of water to fertilize the entire land. This water will be amply supplied in both summer and winter.[3]

The river of "living" waters will heal the Dead Sea, allowing a great multitude of fish to thrive in waters that were once so thick with minerals and salt that nothing could live there.[4] For the first time in history, the Dead Sea will be a "living" sea.

Everywhere this river flows a healing will take place. The river will bring life to the desert and fresh water to a thirsty people and earth. The prophets Isaiah and Ezekiel talked of this almost three thousands years ago:

> The wilderness and the solitary place shall be glad for them; and the desert shall rejoice, and blossom as the rose.
>
> It shall blossom abundantly, and rejoice even with joy and singing: the glory of Lebanon shall be given unto it, the excellency of Carmel and Sharon, they shall see the glory of the Lord, and the excellency of our God.
>
> Isaiah 35:1,2

> And it shall come to pass, that every thing that liveth, which moveth, whithersoever the rivers shall come, shall live: and there shall be a very great multitude of fish, because these waters shall come thither: for they shall be healed; and every thing shall live whither the river cometh.
>
> Ezekiel 47:9

We can see from these passages that the entire physical nature of Israel will be transformed into a land of abundance and growth.

Things will change slowly in the Millennium, but eventually the curse that is on the earth will lessen so that deserts will blossom and fields will yield incredible harvests.[5]

The heavens will change as the moon becomes as bright as the sun. The sun's light will increase sevenfold. However, even the stars will reveal that nature is not the source of life; it is God alone who is the Source.

The light of the Lord and the glory of God will give us the light by which we will see, work, and play.

> Moreover the light of the moon shall be as the light of the sun, and the light of the sun shall be sevenfold, as the light of seven days, in the day that the Lord bindeth up the breach of his people, and healeth the stroke of their wound.
>
> Isaiah 30:26

> The sun shall be no more thy light by day; neither for brightness shall the moon give light unto thee: but the Lord shall be unto thee an everlasting light, and thy God thy glory.

> Thy sun shall no more go down; neither shall thy moon withdraw itself: for the Lord shall be thine everlasting light, and the days of thy mourning shall be ended.
>
> Isaiah 60:19,20

Disease and destruction will become memories as all creatures, men and animals, learn to live together in peace and harmony. The wild beasts will be so tame that the lion will lie down with the lamb. Men will "beat their swords into plowshares, and their spears into pruninghooks" (Isa. 2:4; 11:6-8). War as we now know it will never again darken this planet.

FOLLOW THE PLAN

Human nature, however, will not fall in line with God's plan as easily as nature does. People will still rebel against Christ, but His salvation will be available to redeem those who continue to sin.

Many people who survive the Tribulation and the Battle of Armageddon will be unbelievers. However, when Satan is bound, he will no longer be able to deceive.

> And he laid hold on the dragon, that old serpent, which is the Devil, and Satan, and bound him a thousand years,
>
> And cast him into the bottomless pit, and shut him up, and set a seal upon him, that he should deceive the nations no more, till the thousand years should be fulfilled: and after that he must be loosed a little season.
>
> Revelation 20:2,3

People's eyes will be opened to receive a unique and startling revelation of God's character and glory.

> They shall not hurt nor destroy in all my holy mountain: for the earth shall be full of the knowledge of the Lord, as the waters cover the sea.
>
> Isaiah 11:9

> And, behold, the glory of the God of Israel came from the way of the east: and his voice was like a noise of many waters: and the earth shined with his glory.
>
> Ezekiel 43:2

I believe that at this time most people will change their hearts and give their lives to Jesus.

241

> Thus saith the Lord of hosts; In those days it shall come to pass, that ten men shall take hold out of all languages of the nations, even shall take hold of the skirt of him that is a Jew, saying, We will go with you: for we have heard that God is with you.
>
> Zechariah 8:23

The phrase "take hold of the skirt" refers to a gesture that was naturally used to earnestly request assistance and protection.[6] But some people will continue to deny Christ and live in sin. Yet everyone living during the Millennium will be blessed because the devil will be bound, but they will still have to make the choice to follow God and obey His Word.

In today's world it is still popular to say, "The devil made me do it." The truth is that although he deceives and tries to destroy us, Satan does not make us do anything. We make the choice to rebel against God and reject His Word. The people in the Millennium will also make the choice to sin but without the luxury of saying, "The devil made me do it," because he will not be around to lead anyone into temptation.

Christians in the Millennium will receive the tremendous blessing of salvation in its fullest form. Christ will give them true inner peace, love, righteousness, and complete physical healing.[7]

Long life will be restored to people to the length of life that was common in the Old Testament. Isaiah 65:20 says a child "dies," or becomes an adult, at the age of 100. Lifespans will probably reach to 900 or 1,000 years. However, death will not be eradicated at this time.

We saw that the population of the earth will diminish drastically in the Tribulation and Battle of Armageddon, but during the Millennium it will increase rapidly.

> And God blessed them, and God said unto them, Be fruitful, and multiply, and replenish the earth, and subdue it: and have dominion over the fish of the sea, and over the fowl of the air, and over every living thing that moveth upon the earth.
>
> Genesis 1:28

This "baby boom" proves that people will still fall in love, get married, and raise families during the Millennium in the way God planned when He created man.

CHRIST'S PERFECT GOVERNMENT

The first thing that Jesus will do when He sets up His earthly kingdom will be to assemble the people together. His angels will gather His people from earth and heaven so He can sanctify this incredible congregation of flesh-and-blood humans and glorified saints as they enter into the Millennium with Him.

The word millennium isn't a fancy theological word; it is simply a Latin term that means a thousand years and refers to the length of time that Christ and His saints will rule and reign over the earth.[8]

The saints (who arrived with Christ on white horses and received glorified bodies and minds when they were raptured or resurrected) will reign with Jesus as kings and priests and help Him guide the nations, bringing a perfect form of government to the world.

And I saw thrones, and they sat upon them, and judgment was given unto them: and I saw the souls of them that were beheaded for the witness of Jesus, and for the word of God, and which had not worshipped the beast, neither his image, neither had received his mark upon their foreheads, or in their hands; and they lived and reigned with Christ a thousand years.

Revelation 20:4

God will head this world government through Christ.

I saw in the night visions, and, behold, one like the Son of man came with the clouds of heaven, and came to the Ancient of days, and they brought him near before him.

And there was given him dominion, and glory, and a kingdom, that all people, nations, and languages, should serve him: his dominion is an everlasting dominion, which shall not pass away, and his kingdom that which shall not be destroyed.

Daniel 7:13,14

Christ will reign over the world from the temple in Jerusalem.[9] God's purpose through this government will be to restore a righteous and eternal government on earth as He originally planned.[10]

And David my servant shall be king over them; and they all shall have one shepherd: they shall also walk in my judgments, and observe my statures, and do them.

And they shall dwell in the land that I have given unto Jacob my servant, wherein your fathers have dwelt; and they shall dwell therein, even they, and their children, and their children's children for ever: and my servant David shall be their prince for ever.

Moreover I will make a covenant of peace with them; it shall be an everlasting covenant with them: and I will place them, and multiply them, and will set my sanctuary in the midst of them for evermore.

My tabernacle also shall be with them: yea, I will be their God, and they shall be my people.

And the heathen shall know that I the Lord do sanctify Israel, when my sanctuary shall be in the midst of them for evermore.

Ezekiel 37:24-28

Many Bible scholars agree that this passage literally refers to King David, in his glorified body, ruling over all Israel under Christ during the Millennium." For example, Keil and Delitzsch wrote in their Bible commentary on the Old Testament, "...The union of the Israelites, when brought back to their land, is accomplished by God giving them in David a king who will so rule the reunited people that they will not be divided any more into two peoples and two kingdoms...."[12]

The twelve apostles will be included in this new government. Each will rule over one tribe. In the same way the disciples "suffered with a suffering Jesus," so will they "reign with a reigning Jesus."[13]

And Jesus said unto them, Verily I say unto you, That ye which have followed me, in the regeneration when the Son of man shall sit in the throne of his glory, ye also shall sit upon twelve thrones, judging the twelve tribes of Israel.

Matthew 19:28

The Jews who were redeemed during the Battle of Armageddon will become the head of all nations under the Messiah:

> For the Lord thy God blesseth thee, as he promised thee: and thou shalt lend unto many nations, but thou shalt not borrow; and *thou shalt reign over many nations, but they shall not reign over thee.*
>
> Deuteronomy 15:6

During the Millennium, God will restore the years that the locust ate by giving the Jews all the land and blessings He had promised to Abraham, Isaac, Jacob, and David.[14]

At the beginning of the Millennium, Israel will receive all the land east of the Mediterranean Sea and Nile River and west of the Euphrates River. Generally, the new Israel will cover the land that is now Egypt, Sudan, Ethiopia, Somalia, Saudi Arabia, Oman, the United Arab Emirates, Kuwait, Iraq, Syria, Turkey, Jordan, and Israel. The Gentile nations will receive land according to God's plan, and all nations will be required to send representatives to Jerusalem once a year to acknowledge Christ at the Feast of Tabernacles. Those countries that are not represented at the feast will be cursed with a plague and drought.

> And it shall come to pass, that every one that is left of all the nations which came against Jerusalem shall even go up from year to year to worship the King, the Lord of hosts, and to keep the feast of tabernacles.
>
> And it shall be, that whoso will not come up of all the families of the earth unto Jerusalem to worship the King, the Lord of hosts, even upon them shall be no rain.

And if the family of Egypt go not up, and come not, that have no rain; there shall be the plague, wherewith the Lord will smite the heathen that come not up to keep the feast of tabernacles.

This shall be the punishment of Egypt, and the punishment of all nations that come not up to keep the feast of tabernacles.

Zechariah 14:16-19

The Levitical priesthood will be reestablished and serve in the millennial temple.[15] They will prepare all the former offerings, feasts, and rituals of the temple as a form of worship, showing people Christ's redeeming work through the pictures of the rituals.[16] This will be similar to us taking communion.

The Jews will evangelize the nations in a one-world religion that blesses all nations.[17] The blessings of Christ's perfect government will be the peace, justice, and prosperity that fill the earth.[18]

FORMER AND LATTER RAINS

Something that I consider extremely exciting is that when the Millennium begins, the Holy Spirit will be poured out on all flesh with tremendous power.

And it shall come to pass afterward, that I will pour out my spirit upon all flesh; and your sons and your daughters shall prophesy, your old men shall dream dreams, your young men shall see visions:

And also upon the servants and upon the handmaids in those days will I pour out my spirit.

Joel 2:28,29

Joel refers to this outpouring of the Holy Spirit as the former and latter rains.

> Be glad then, ye children of Zion, and rejoice in the Lord your God: for he hath given you the former rain moderately, and he will cause to come down for you the rain, the former rain, and the latter rain in the first month.
>
> Joel 2:23

He uses this description because Israel's economy and society were primarily based on agriculture. In the natural, the former and latter rains marked the harvest timetable.

The former rain was the moderate spring rain that came at planting time to give the seeds moisture to germinate and grow. The latter rains came in the fall in large amounts to make the vegetables and fruit multiply and grow large. Together, these combinations of rain made a bountiful harvest that blessed people throughout the year.

I believe that the spiritual meaning of the passage refers to the glory of the Lord in the Old and New Testaments. The former rain is God's Spirit poured out in the Old Testament; the latter rain is His glory in the New Testament.[19] You and I are actually living in the latter rain, which began on the day of Pentecost. This "rain," or glory, is poured out upon us so we can reap a bountiful harvest of souls.

One Greek lexicon describes *glory* as "magnificence, excellence, preeminence, dignity, grace...majesty...." It goes on to say that it is "the glorious condition of blessedness into which is appointed and promised that true Christians shall enter after their Saviour's return from heaven."[20]

At the beginning of the Millennium, something unique and wonderful will happen because the latter and former rains[21] will come together and pour out upon all people, showering every one with the glory of the Lord as He was, is, and will be. In other words, His very presence, the very essence of Himself, will be manifested on the earth.

The saints of the Old and New Testaments will enter the millennial reign of the Lord together. They will experience the glory that was revealed to Abraham, shone on Moses' face, guided and protected the Israelites by the pillar of fire and the cloud, and filled the wilderness tabernacle and the temple.

In addition, they will feel the power of God that was manifested on the day of Pentecost and has been pouring out for nearly 2,000 years. This is very exciting to me! I love the way the Holy Spirit moves on people today; it's hard to imagine how much better it can get. The presence of the Lord will truly be incredible during the Millennium.

SATAN UNLEASHED

And when the thousand years are expired, Satan shall be loosed out of his prison,

And shall go out to deceive the nations which are in the four quarters of the earth, Gog and Magog, to gather them together to battle: the number of whom is as the sand of the sea.

And they went up on the breadth of the earth, and compassed the camp of the saints about, and the beloved city: and fire came down from God out of heaven, and devourer them.

> And the devil that deceived them was cast into the lake of fire and brimstone, where the beast and the false prophet are, and shall be tormented day and night for ever and ever.
>
> Revelation 20:7-10

It almost seems a pity that after the world rests in such a long period of peace, at the end of the thousand years Satan, the enemy of peace, will be unleashed and allowed to roam the earth again for a while. But it appears to be necessary as God Himself tells John in Revelation 20:3, "...he must be loosed a little season."

Perhaps it will be to show how even a thousand-year imprisonment didn't change him. Or it may be to let the nations see that even after living in holy obedience all that time in a happy and peaceful world, they will still be unable to stand without the help and grace of God.[22]

It is obvious from Satan's actions after he is set free that his fury will have only grown during the Millennium, because he will set out to finish what he started at the Battle of Armageddon. He will gather the sinners and rebels who remain and his army will march again until they reach Jerusalem. But before anything can happen, fire will come down from heaven and devour the soldiers. God then will throw Satan into the Lake of Fire, where he will spend eternity in pain and torment.

JUDGMENT DAY

With Satan and the people who denied Christ cast off the earth, God will begin His final judgment of mankind. All the people who had denied Christ will be resurrected from the dead in order to stand before God's Great White Throne.

God will look in the Lamb's Book of Life to find the name of each person who stands before His throne. This Book of Life contains only the names of Christ's followers. Those who are not found in the book will be judged for the things they had done in life, based upon that which is written in the Book of Works, and then they will be thrown into the Lake of Fire.

> But the rest of the dead lived not again until the thousand years were finished. This is the first resurrection.
>
> Revelation 20:5

> And I saw a great white throne, and him that sat on it, from whose face the earth and the heaven fled away; and there was found no place for them.
>
> And I saw the dead, small and great, stand before God; and the books were opened: and another book was opened, which is the book of life: and the dead were judged out of those things which were written in the books, according to their works.
>
> And the sea gave up the dead which were in it; and death and hell delivered up the dead which were in them: and they were judged every man according to their works.
>
> And death and hell were cast into the lake of fire. This is the second death.
>
> And whosoever was not found written in the book of life was cast into the lake of fire.
>
> Revelation 20:11-15

As we see in verse 14, death and hell will be cast into the Lake of Fire and never darken the face of the earth again.

The saints will not participate in the Great White Throne Judgment because we have already received eternal life.

> Blessed and holy is he that hath part in the first resurrection: on such the second death hath no power, but they shall be priests of God and of Christ, and shall reign with him a thousand years.
>
> Revelation 20:6

The "second death" referred to here is the death that the wicked will face after judgment.[23] In fact, only they will take part in that judgment. But, as this next passage states, the righteous (the children of God) will be rewarded.

> When the Son of man shall come in his glory, and all the holy angels with him, then shall he sit upon the throne of his glory:
>
> And before him shall be gathered all nations: and he shall separate them one from another, as a shepherd divideth his sheep from the goats:
>
> And he shall set the sheep on his right hand, but the goats on the left.
>
> Then shall the King say unto them on his right hand, Come, ye blessed of my Father, inherit the kingdom prepared for you from the foundation of the world:
>
> Then shall he say also unto them on the left hand, Depart from me, ye cursed, into everlasting fire, prepared for the devil and his angels:
>
> And these shall go away into everlasting punishment: but the righteous into life eternal.
>
> Matthew 25:31-34,41,46

We will appear before "the judgment seat of Christ, that every one may receive the things done in his body, according to that he hath done" (2 Cor. 5:10). However, at the Judgment Seat of Christ, God will not recompense His children for their iniquities. We will only be recompensed for our "good" deeds so that we will receive rewards.[24]

ALL THINGS NEW

For, behold, I create new heavens and a new earth: and the former shall not be remembered, nor come into mind.

But be ye glad and rejoice for ever in that which I create: for, behold, I create Jerusalem a rejoicing, and her people a joy.

And I will rejoice in Jerusalem, and joy in my people: and the voice of weeping shall be no more heard in her, nor the voice of crying.

Isaiah 65:17-19

Now that the devil, his angels and followers, and all the bodies of the wicked have been removed from the earth and seas, the curse and wages of sin will be finally lifted from man and earth.

God will dwell with men on earth, where there will be no more tears, death, sorrow, curse, crying, pain, or night. Sin and death will be gone. The whole plan of redemption will now be complete.

And God shall wipe away all tears from their eyes; and there shall be no more death, neither sorrow, nor crying, neither shall there be any more pain: for the former things are passed away.

Revelation 21:4

And there shall be no more curse: but the throne of God and of the Lamb shall be in it; and his servants shall serve him:

And there shall be no night there; and they need no candle, neither light of the sun; for the Lord God giveth them light: and they shall reign for ever and ever.

Revelation 22:3,5

The new heaven and earth will not be the result of an unrecorded catastrophe that occurs after the Great White Throne Judgment. They will be the result of the process of restoration and regeneration that will be started with the Tribulation and completed by Christ during the Millennium.

It is not possible for Christ to fail. So, to say that God destroys the world and creates a new one, even after Christ redeemed it, is wrong. The term *passed away* in Revelation 21:4 doesn't suggest destruction; it is a redemption expression that suggests former things are behind, have gone by, or are in the past.[25]

Besides, why would trees applaud and mountains and hills break into song, as this next passage says, unless they had not once known the weight of the curse of sin and death and then felt that incredible burden lift?

For ye shall go out with joy, and be led forth with peace: the mountains and the hills shall break forth before you into singing, and all the trees of the field shall clap their hands.

Instead of the thorn shall come up the fir tree, and instead of the brier shall come up the myrtle tree: and it shall be to the Lord for a name, for an everlasting sign that shall not be cut off.

Isaiah 55:12,13

This new world will be one of joy and godly substance, not a new creation. It will be a world where there are no more thorns or thistles, no locusts, plagues, blight, mildew, or weeds.

THE CAPITAL OF THE UNIVERSE

Revelation 21 and 22 describe the New Jerusalem, which will come down from God out of heaven, casting down His glory over the world and giving it light. The city will have a great wall with twelve gates of pearl. It will be made of gold, with walls of jasper, decorations of precious stones, and streets of gold.

The River of Life will flow from the thrones of God and Christ. The Tree of Life, once in the Garden of Eden, will stand in the midst of the street on either side of the river. It will yield its fruit every month, and its leaves will heal the nations.

Holy Jerusalem will be the home of the bride of Christ, the saints whose names are written in the Lamb's Book of Life. The saints will come to live here after the Millennium to fulfill the promise Jesus gave us when He said, "In my Father's house are many mansions... I go to prepare a place for you" (John 14:2).

This city will be the capital of the universe because God's throne is in it. Its citizens will be the kings and priests who give the world the benefits of the water of life and the leaves of the tree of life.

From the creation of the world to its restoration, God has continued to show us that He loves us and wants us to accept His salvation. He does not want us to try to change, but to accept the love and redemption from Christ that will change us. We are powerless to make ourselves sinless, perfect, and holy; only Christ in His redemptive work can accomplish this. What a wonderful message of hope, salvation, and redemption God has given us through His Son and His Word!

In the world things may seem bad and getting worse—going from gloom to doom. But God's message to us is that there is Someone—our Savior, our Redeemer—who is tossing us a rope and pulling us out. He is extending to us a lifeline and is our means of rescue and release from the horrors to come. The Scriptures and events we've looked at in this book and the terrible situations going on everywhere are pointing the way to the Second Coming, when we will see Him face to face.

Remember, in a world that seems out of control, we have a big God. Let's not get caught up looking at the end-time terror tactics of Satan, but at exalting God's Son Jesus and watching for the day of His return!

CONCLUSION

The wicked plotteth against the just, and gnasheth upon him with his teeth.

The Lord shall laugh at him: for he seeth that his day is coming.

Psalm 37:12,13

This is a message that God strongly impressed upon me to share with you. I hope that you've caught every bit of it because any fear a believer may be struggling with over the last days can be resolved through understanding Bible prophecy. That's why this book is designed to make end-time prophecy clear for you.

We're in the end times, and there are circumstances and events that are going to go on that can be unsettling. But God has a strategy in all the mess—a strategy of what He wants to do in us, through us, and for us. I've tried to present it to you in these pages, along with the "God keys" to attaining it, to encourage you that you can boldly take a step of faith and be a part of what God wants to do in this final hour.

It's true that present-day events are causing some to be overcome with fear. Those who don't know the Lord or who don't understand Bible prophecy are living in darkness and have no hope for a bright future. But we who believe have the future promise of the Rapture and a glorious home in heaven. This should truly make all the difference in the way we live our life in this last hour.

God loves His children tremendously and desires to encourage and awaken us to the events of the end times. We are actually part of His divine plan.

As born-again believers, we do have a place in these last days that is attainable; we have a purpose to watch, to pray, and to win souls to Jesus. We can't afford to do stupid things, as sleeping around or getting sloppy in our walk with God, because we're going to see the greatest miracles of people coming to Jesus that we've ever seen before. We're going to see nations shaken as we've never seen before, and it's God's strategy for us to be part of it. But if we get sloppy, we're going to miss it.

God has chosen us to live in this hour to watch the signs of the times and participate in bringing His divine plan to pass. As Christians, we can choose to tune in to the message God has presented in prophecy or ignore His Word. I hope that this book has helped you to make the right choice and inspired you not to give up.

In these pages I have shared with you how to fill your spirit with God's Word, how to open your spiritual eyes (with the help of the Holy Spirit), how to uncover the signs that will help you to watch for Jesus' return, and how to know God's leading for you down the road to the Rapture. What a time of restoration that will be!

God is going to reverse the things the devil meant for our harm and turn them for our good.

Remember, the entire end-time story, including the Rapture, is one of restoration. The events of the last days bring the story of man's sinfulness full circle. From the beginning, when Adam and Eve sinned, God set up a plan to protect His fallen children, to bring them back to His holy embrace. Through the events of the Tribulation and Armageddon, God will give the world back to its original owner (mankind) and return it to its original state. During the Rapture of the church and the return of Jesus Christ people will receive glorified bodies; they will never again experience sin, pain, hunger, sadness, or death.

God has chosen to live in us, by His Spirit, but we can also look forward to living with Him where we will have total redemption of our body. One day, the last trumpet will sound, the dead in Christ will rise, and we will be "caught up" to meet Him in the air. Heaven is a prepared place for a prepared and watching people.

The end times, the last days, the final hour, is real. But God is here with us, and it's temporary. Knowing that He is with us every step of the way makes it wonderful. He is going to take us through, and we're going to be victorious!

ENDNOTES

Chapter 1

[1] Thayer and Smith, *The KJV New Testament Greek Lexicon*, "Greek Lexicon entry for Kraipale," s.v. "surfeiting," available from <http://www.biblestudytools.net/Lexicons/Greek/grk. cgi?number=2897&version=kj>.

[2] Ibid., "Greek Lexicon entry for Agrupneo," s.v. "watch," available from <http://www.biblestudytools.net/Lexicons/Greek/grk. cgi?number=69&vers ion=kjv>.

[3] Charlton G. Laird, *Webster's New World Thesaurus*, (Collins World, 1971), p. 234, s.v. "follow."

[4] Tommy Tenney, *God Chasers: "My Soul Follows Hard After Thee"* (Destiny Image, 1999).

[5] Thayer and Smith, "Greek Lexicon entry for Harpazo," s.v. "caught up," 1 Thessalonians 4:17, available from <http://www.biblestudytools.net/ Lexicons/Greek/grk.cgi ?number=726&version=kjv>.

Chapter 3

[1] "The eminent spiritual blessings of Shem are fulfilled in the Messiah, who came from the line of Shem (cf. Rom. 9:3-5)." *New Unger's Bible Dictionary*, originally published by Moody Press of Chicago, Illinois. Copyright© 1988; s.v. "SHEM." Used by permission.

[2] Melchizedek was a godly priest who went out to congratulate Abraham on his victory. He brought food and drink to Abraham and his tired men and blessed them. In return, Abraham gave him

a tenth of the spoils taken from the enemy. Based on a definition in *Unger's*, s.v. "MELCHLZEDEK."

[3] Ibid., S. V. "LORD WILL PROVIDE."

[4] *Adam Clarke's Commentary* (Electronic Database: Biblesoft, 1996), "Esther 1:11." All rights reserved.

Chapter 4

[1] Revelation 2:20-24.

[2] Revelation 20:10.

[3] *Jamieson, Fausset, and Brown Commentary*, (Electronic Database: Biblesoft, 1997), s.v. "Genesis 3:14-15." All rights reserved.

[4] Ibid.

[5] Adam Clarke, s.v. "Genesis 3:15."

[6] *Barnes' Notes*, by Albert Barnes, D.D. (Electronic Database: Biblesoft, 1997), s.v. "Colossians 2:15." All rights reserved.

[7] Unger's, S.V. "SHEM."

[8] *John Wesley's Explanatory Notes on the Whole Bible*, s.v. "The Book of Genesis, Chapter 9," Genesis 9:27; available from <http://bible. cross- walk.com/Commentaries/WesleysExplanatoryNotes/wes. cgi?book=ge&chapter=009>.

[9] *Keil and Delitzsch Commentary on the Old Testament: New Updated Edition* (Electronic Database: Hendrickson Publishers, Inc., 1996), s.v. "Genesis 49:8-10." Used by permission. All rights reserved.

[10] Unger's, s.v. "SHILOH."

[11] Isaiah 9:6.

[12] *Barnes' Notes*, s.v. "Revelation 5:5."

[13] Jamieson, Fausset and Brown, s.v. "Genesis 49:8-10."

[14] Adam Clarke, s.v. "1 Corinthians 6:2."

Chapter 5

[1] *Merriam-Webster's Collegiate Dictionary*, 10th ed. (New York: Merriam Webster, Inc., 1998), s.v. "anti."

2   James E. Strong, "Greek Dictionary of the New Testament" in *Strong's Exhaustive Concordance of the Bible* (Nashville: Abingdon, 1890), p. 78, entry #5547, s.v. "Christ."

3   " ... Many evangelical interpreters see here a type of Antichrist and his conflict with Christ and his people in the end time. This may very well be...." *The Wycliffe Bible Commentary*, edited by Charles E. Pfeiffer and Everett F. Harrison (Electronic Database: Moody Press, 1962), s.v. "Daniel 8:9- 14." All rights reserved.

4   Based on a notes section from Spiros Zodhiates, *The Complete Word Dictionary: Old Testament* (Chattanooga: AMG Publishers, 1994), p. 2101, s.v. "Daniel 2:31-45."

5   "[His legs of iron] The Roman government. [His feet part of iron and part of clay.] The same, mixed with the barbaric nations, and divided into ten kingdoms...." Adam Clarke, s.v. "Daniel 2:33."

6   Jamieson, Fausset, and Brown, s.v. "Daniel 2:34.

7   Daniel 7:1-28; 8:2-27.

8   Spiros Zodhiates, *The Complete Word Dictionary: Old Testament*, p. 2133, s.v. "[Daniel] 11:21-35."

9   R. Laird Harris, Gleason L. Archer, Jr., Bruce K. Waltke, *Theological Wordbook of the Old Testament*, Vol. 1, (Chicago, Illinois: Moody Press, 1980), pp. 98-99, entry #224a, s.v. "bazah (vile person)," Daniel 11:21.

10 *International Standard Bible Encyclopaedia*, original James Orr 1915 Edition (Electronic Database: Biblesoft, 1995-1996), s.v. "MAGOG."

11 Based on information from notes in Spiros Zodhiates, Th.D., *The Complete Word Dictionary: New Testament*, (Chattanooga: AMG Publishers, 1992), p. 681, s.v. "[2 Thessalonians] 2:3-9."

12 *The Life Application Bible Notes and Bible Helps* (Tyndale House Publishers, Inc., 1991).

13 Spiros Zodhiates, *The Complete Word Dictionary: New Testament*, p. 834, s.v. "[Revelation] 13:1-18."

14 Based on information from *Frequently Asked Questions Answered by Don Stewart*, "Why Did God Use the King of Babylon and the King of Tyre To Illustrate the Fall of Satan?" from the Blue Letter Bible Web site available from <http://www.blueletterbible.org/faq/nbi/83.htmb.

15 *International Standard Encyclopedia*, s.v. "PERDITION."

16 Keil and Delitzsch, s.v. "Psalm 55:1."

17 Thayer and Smith, *The KJV New Testament Greek Lexicon*, "Greek Lexicon entry for Diabolos," entry #1228, s.v. "a devil," available from <http://www.biblestudytools. net/Lexicons/Greek/grk. cgi?number=1228&version=kjv>.

18 *Matthew Henry's Commentary on the Whole Bible: New Modern Edition* (Electronic Database: Hendrickson Publishers, Inc., 1991), s.v. "John 6:60-71, Christ's discourse with His disciples."

19 " ...All the curses written in God's book now came into his [Judas'] bowels like water, and like oil into his bones, as was foretold concerning him (Ps. 109:18,19), and drove him to this desperate shift, for the escaping of a hell within him, to leap into that before him, which was but the perfection and perpetuity of this horror and despair. He throws himself into the fire, to avoid the flame; but miserable is the case when a man must go to hell for ease." Ibid, s.v. "Matthew 27:1-10, The repentance of Judas."

20 Luke 8:30-31; Revelation 20:1-3.

21 Based on notes at the beginning of the book of Habakkuk and in the notes section in Spiros Zodhiates' *The Complete Word Dictionary: Old Testament*, p. 2215, s.v. "[Habakkuk] 1:2-11."

Chapter 6

1 John 8:12.

2 Brown, Driver, Briggs and Gesenius, *The KJV Old Testament Hebrew Lexicon*, "Hebrew Lexicon entry for 'az,'" entry #5794, s.v. "fierce," available from <http://www.biblesrudytools.net/Lexicons/Hebrew/heb.cgi?number=5794&version=kjv>.

3 *Theological Wordbook of the Old Testament,* Vol. II, p. 659, entry #1596a, s.v. "az (fierce)," Daniel 8:23.

4 Based on information from *Barnes' Notes,* s.v. "Daniel 8:23."

5 Ibid.

6 Wycliffe, s.v. "Daniel 8:23-27."

7 Adam Clarke, s.v. "Daniel 8:3."

8 Ibid, s.v. "Daniel 8:5."

9 Ibid.

Chapter 7

1 " ...Some things in this prediction concerning Antiochus are alluded to in the New-Testament predictions of the antichrist...." *Matthew Henry's Commentary on the Whole Bible,* s.v. "Daniel 11:21-45."

2 Isaiah 14:12-14; Ezekiel 28:12-18.

3 Wycliffe, s.v. "Revelation 17:1-12."

4 Genesis 4:1-7.

5 *International Standard Encyclopedia,* s.v. "BABEL, BABYLON."

6 Matthew Henry, s.v. "Genesis 12:1-3, The Call of Abram."

7 Joshua 6:18,19.

8 Daniel 1:1.

9 Daniel 3:1.

10 *Theological Wordbook of the Old Testament,* Vol. Il, p. 955, entry #2459b, s.v. "abomination," Daniel 12:11.

11 Revelation 7:9-17; 14:1-5.

12 *Merriam-Webster OnLine Dictionary,* s.v. "geopolitics"; available from <http://www.m-w.com>.

13 Strong's, entry #6643, p. 98, s.v. "Daniel 8:9."

14 "Ezekiel 38,39.

[15] Genesis 10:2,5.

[16] Daniel 2,7.

[17] Genesis 10:7. "

[18] Genesis 10:4.

[19] Ezekiel 38:13.

[20] Ephesians 2:2.

Chapter 8

[1] Wycliffe, s.v. "Revelation 13:18."

[2] *The KJV Old Testament Hebrew Lexicon*, "Hebrew Lexicon entry for Tav," entry #8420, s.v. "a mark" available from <http://www.biblestudyrools.net/ Lexicons/Hebrew/heb. cgi?number=842O&version=kjv>.

[3] *International Standard Bible Encylopaedia*, s.v. "MARK."

[4] Ibid.

[5] Joseph A. Seiss, The Apocalypse: Exposition of the Book of Revelation (Biblesoft: Electronic Database, 1998), s.v. "Revelation 12:1-2," "Revelation 13:13-18."

[6] Warren W. Wiersbe, *The Essential Everyday Bible Commentary* (Nashville: Thomas Nelson Publishers, 1991), s.v. "Revelation 13:11-18."

Chapter 9

[1] Matthew 5:13.

[2] Matthew 18:18.

Chapter 10

[1] Strong's, "Greek Dictionary of the New Testament," p. 16, entry #726, s.v. "shall be caught up," 1 Thessalonians 4:17.

[2] Ibid, "Hebrew and Chaldee Dictionary," p. 67, entry #4422, s.v. "shall be delivered," Daniel 12:1.

3   Based on notes from Warren W. Wiersbe, p. 1175, s.v. "Daniel 12:1."

4   Based on a definition from *Merriam-Webster's Online Dictionary*, "rapture."

5   *University of Notre Dame Latin Dictionary and Grammar Aid*, s.v. "rapere," available from <http:/www.nd.edu/-archives/latgramm. htm>.

6   1 Thessalonians. 4:16; Revelation. 4:1; 6:1,2.

7   Strong's, "Greek Dictionary of the New Testament," p. 17, entry #823, s.v. "a moment," 1 Corinthians 15:52.

8   Joseph A. Seiss, s.v. "Revelation 12:5."

9   Revelation 12:5.

10   Revelation 12:1.

11   Luke 10:19.

12   Matthew Henry, s.v. "Revelation 3:14-22."

13   Based on information from Wycliffe, s.v. "Revelation 12:7-9."

14   Ezekiel 28:18; Daniel 8:10-13; Revelation 12:7-10.

15   Barnes' Notes, s.v. "Revelation 12:16."

Chapter 11

1   Strong's, "Greek Dictionary of the New Testament," p. 36, entry #2347, s.v. "tribulation," Matthew 24:29.

2   *Merriam- Webster's OnLine Dictionary*, s.v. "tribulation."

3   "...God-Messiah will 'anoint' or consecrate with His presence the holy place at Jerusalem after its pollution by Antichrist, of which the feast of dedication after the pollution by Antiochus was a type (Jer. 3:16-17; Ezek. 37:27-28)." Jamieson, Fausset, and Brown, s.v. "Daniel 9:24."

4   Strong's, "Greek Dictionary of the New Testament," p. 9, entry #165, s.v. "world," Matthew 13:40.

5   John 12:32; 16:7-11.

6 Revelation 6:9-11; 7:9,14; 14:12-13.

7 Matthew 24:29-31,38,39; Luke 21:25,26; Revelation 6:12-17.

8 Matthew 24:21; Revelation 2:22.

9 Revelation 7:5-8.

10 " ...that 12,000 chosen in each tribe will be protected from the wrath of Satan and the Antichrist...." Taken from notes section in Spiros Zodhiates' *The Complete Word Dictionary: New Testament,* p. 822, s.v. *"The 144,00,"* Revelation 7, describing the 144,000 servants of God.

11 "...The reign of the antichrist is the reign of harlotry, both literal and spiritual. It is a time when chaste marriage is no more regarded than the worship of the true God...." Joseph A. Seiss, s.v. "Revelation 14:1-5."

12 Exodus 9,10,11.

13 *International Standard Bible Encylopaedia,* s.v. "PLAGUES, OF EGYPT."

14 "Egyptians and probably other nationalities who had married Hebrews, were seeking escape from bondage or were persuaded that there was some advantage to be gained by being on the side of so powerful a deity as Jehovah." Wycliffe, s.v. "Exodus 12:37-39."

15 Matthew 17:1-3.

16 "...They [the two witnesses] are given supernatural power, such as Elijah and Moses had (1 Kings 17:1), to slay their enemies, to cause a drought, to turn water into blood, and to smite the earth with plagues at their will...." Wycliffe, s.v. "Revelation 11 :3-12." Also see Exodus 7:20; 9:23; 2 Kings 1:12.

17 Revelation 11:3.

18 Matthew Henry, s.v. "Revelation 11:3-13, The two witnesses."

Chapter 12
1 Strong's, "Greek Dictionary of the New Testament," p. 39, entry #2556, s.v. "noisome," Revelation 16:2.

2   Ibid, p. 59, entry #4190, s.v. "grievous," Revelation 16:2.

3   *Merriam- Webster's Online Dictionary*, s.v. "wormwood."

4   *International Standard Bible Encylopaedia*, s.v. "GALL."

5   Unger's, S.V. "GODS, FALSE."

6   Strong's "Greek Dictionary of the New Testament," p. 14, entry #623, s.v. "Apollyon," Revelation 9:11.

7   Revelation 16:12-16.

8   Adam Clarke, s.v. "Revelation 10:2."

9   James A. Seiss, s.v. "Revelation 10:1-11."

10   Ephesians 1:11-14; Revelation 10:10.

11   Matthew Henry, s.v. "Revelation 10:8-11, The charge to further prophecy."

Chapter 13

1   *Merriam-Webster's OnLine Dictionary*, s.v. "Armageddon."

2   Revelation 19:15,21.

3   Thayer and Smith, "Greek Lexicon entry for Armageddon," <http://www.biblestudytools.net/Lexicons/Greek/grk. cgi?number=717&ve rsion=kjv>.

4   "A Greek version of the Jewish Scriptures redacted in the 3d and 2d centuries B.C. by Jewish scholars and adopted by Greek-speaking Christians." *Merriam-Webster's OnLine Dictionary*, s.v. "Septuagint."

5   Ibid, s.v. "apocalypse."

6   Based on information from Unger's, s.v. "ARMAGEDDON."

7   Joshua 17:11.

8   Unger's, S.V. "MEGIDDO."

9   Albert Barnes, *Barnes' Notes on the New Testament*, Electronic text and markup: Epiphany Software, 1999.

10   Based on information from Thayer and Smith, "Greek Lexicon entry for Armageddon," entry #717, s.v. "Armageddon,"

<http://www.biblestudy- tools.net/Lexicons/Greek/grk. cgi?number=717&version=kjv>.

[11] Brown, Driver, Briggs and Gesenius, "Hebrew Lexicon entry for Megiddown (Zech. 12:11)," entry #4023, s.v. "Megiddo," available from <http://www.biblestudytooIs.net/Lexicons/Hebrew/heb. cgi?number=4023&version=kjv>.

[12] James Strong, "Hebrew and Chaldee Dictionary," in Strong's Exhaustive Concordance of the Bible (Nashville: Abingdon, 1890), p. 61, entry #4023, s.v. "Megiddo."

[13] Based upon information from Brown, Driver, Briggs and Gesenius, "Hebrew Lexicon entry for Gadad," entry #1413, s.v. "Gadad," available from <http://www.biblestudytools.net/Lexicons/Hebrew/heb.cgi?number=1413&version=kjv>.

[14] Grant R. Jeffery, *Messiah-War in the Middle East and the Road to Armageddon*, Bantam Books, 1992.

[15] Ibid.

[16] Joshua 12:1-24.

[17] 2 Kings 9,10.

[18] Judges 4:1-24.

[19] Based on a definition from Strong's "Hebrew and Chaldee Dictionary," p.30, entry #1766, s.v. "thrust," Joel 2:8.

[20] Ibid, p. 48, entry #3092, s.v. "Jehoshaphat," Joel 3:12.

[21] Genesis 4:3-7.

[22] Strong's, "Greek Dictionary of the New Testament," p. 47, entry #3340, s.v. "Repent," Matthew 4:17.

[23] Ibid, p. 47, entry #3338, s.v. "repent," Matthew 27:3.

[24] Matthew Henry, s.v. "Revelation 19:11-21, The triumph of the saints."

Chapter 14

[1] Revelation 19:9.

[2] Revelation 19:7,8.

3   Revelation 19:11-13.

4   Revelation 19:14.

5   Barnes' Notes, s.v. "Matthew 3:12."

6   Based on a definition from *Webster's II*, s.v. "Edomites."

7   Genesis 19:24,28; Isaiah 13:19; Jeremiah 51:47-49.

8   Barnes' Notes, s.v. "Revelation 19:17."

9   Isaiah 24:21,22; Matthew 13:41-43; 25:41; Revelation 19:20,21; 20:1-3.

10 Ezekiel 39:4,5,17-20.

11 Based on information from the *International Standard Bible Encyclopaedia*, s.v. "HAMON-GOG."

12 Ezekiel 39:9,10.

Chapter 15

1   Ezekiel 39:11-14.

2   Adam Clarke, s.v. "Zechariah 14:8."

3   Wycliffe, s.v. "Zechariah 14:8."

4   Ezekiel 47:8,10.

5   Joel 2:22; 3:18; Amos 9:13-15.

6   Adam Clarke, s.v. "Zechariah 8:23."

7   Isaiah 9:7; 11:5; 32:1-3; 33:24; 35:5,6; Ezekiel 36:25,26.

8   Based on a definition from Unger's, s.v. "MILLENNIUM."

9   Isaiah 2:2-4; Zechariah 6:12,13.

10 Isaiah 9:6,7; 11:1-5; Daniel 2:44; Luke 1:32,33; Revelation 11:15.

11 Wycliffe, s.v. "Ezekial 37:16-25."

12 *Keil & Delitzsch Commentary on the Old Testament*, s.v. "Ezekiel 37:15-28."

13 Based on information from Matthew Henry, s.v. "Matthew 19:23-30, The recompense of Christ's followers."

14   Genesis 13:14,15; 15:17; Isaiah 60:21; Joel 2:25.

15   Isaiah 66:21.

16   Ezekiel 43:19-27.

17   Isaiah 2:2-4.

18   Isaiah 29:17-20; Jeremiah 31:27,28.

19   Barnes' Notes, s.v. "Joel 2:23."

20   Thayer and Smith, "Greek Lexicon entry for Doxa," entry #1391, s.v. "glory," available from <http://www.biblestudytools.net/ Lexicons/Greek/ grk.cgi ?number= 1391&version=kjv>.

21   Joel 2:23.

22   Joseph A. Seiss, s.v. "Revelation 20:7-10."

23   Barnes' Notes, s.v. "Revelation 20:6."

24   Matthew 25:35-40.

25   Strong's, "Greek Dictionary of the New Testament," p. 14, entry #565, s.v. "are passed away," Revelation 21:4.

OTHER BOOKS BY MARILYN HICKEY

PRAYER OF SALVATION

God loves you—no matter who you are, no matter what your past. God loves you so much that He gave His one and only begotten Son for you. The Bible tells us that "...whoever believes in Him shall not perish but have eternal life" (John 3:16 NIV). Jesus laid down His life and rose again so that we could spend eternity with Him in heaven and experience His absolute best on earth. If you would like to receive Jesus into your life, say the following prayer out loud and mean it from your heart.

Heavenly Father, I come to You admitting that I am a sinner. Right now, I choose to turn away from sin, and I ask You to cleanse me of all unrighteousness. I believe that Your Son, Jesus, died on the cross to take away my sins. I also believe that He rose again from the dead so that I might be forgiven of my sins and made righteous through faith in Him. I call upon the name of Jesus Christ to be the Savior and Lord of my life. Jesus, I choose to follow You and ask that You fill me with the power of the Holy Spirit. I declare that right now I am a child of God. I am free from sin and full of the righteousness of God. I am saved in Jesus' name. Amen.

If you prayed this prayer to receive Jesus Christ as your Savior for the first time, please contact us on the Web at **www.harrisonhouse.com** to receive a free book.

Or you may write to us at
Harrison House • 167 Walnut Bottom Rd • Shippensburg, PA 17257

Fast. Easy.
Convenient.

For the latest Harrison House product information and author news, look no further than your computer. All the details on our powerful, life-changing products are just a click away. New releases, E-mail subscriptions, testimonies, monthly specials—find it all in one place. Visit harrisonhouse.com today!

harrisonhouse

The Harrison House Vision

Proclaiming the truth and the power

Of the Gospel of Jesus Christ

With excellence;

Challenging Christians to

Live victoriously,

Grow spiritually,

Know God intimately.